It Takes A Sense Of Humour

A twinless twin's journey of loss, love, and triumph over hidden handicaps

Patty O'Leary Emry

Edited by
Greg Dean Emry
and Bernice Clever

Produced by:

FriesenPress

Suite 300 – 852 Fort Street
Victoria, BC, Canada V8W 1H8

www.friesenpress.com

Distributed to the trade by The Ingram Book Company

Table of Contents

Advance Praise

"Patty's book is an **intriguing** inspirational story of hope and motivation to anyone who on a daily basis must adapt their health and lifestyle to live and flourish."

Dr. O'Leary - Denver, Colorado

—

"I have known Patty Emry for over 30 years; she is a woman of faith, courage and determination! For most of this time I was not aware of Patty's day to day struggles. This book is a realistic journey through her life and depicts how she turns her days and history into a thriving success.

The medical descriptions are unflinching and vivid, giving the narrative a raw authenticity that is powerful and compelling. A must read for anyone who faces similar challenges or for anyone that wants to know how to live with gusto!"

Lynette Jones RN – Vancouver, British Columbia

—

"Patty's determination to be successful in all aspects of her life has allowed her to overcome her physical challenges. She has taken what could have been a handicap and transformed it into her unique personality that has been able to remain optimistic despite adversity. She has been an inspiration to me and I am proud to call her my friend. My admiration extends to her husband and her family who have supported her through the tough times and have enveloped Patty with their love."

Jan Martin – Physiotherapist – Lions Gate Hospital North Vancouver British Columbia

—

"Before reading this book, I had thought I understood Patty's medical issues; now I have a much better appreciation of the incredible challenges she has faced and overcome! The fact that she has accomplished so much during her life and done so with such a positive attitude is testament to the power of the human spirit in the face of adversity. A must read for anyone who is in need of inspiration."

Peter Martin – Read the book – long time friend, Vancouver British Columbia

Introduction

At the sweet age of 63, I am blessed to be alive. Every day when I wake up I ask myself, 'Sweet, what will I accomplish today? And, halleluiah, who can I make smile today?' I probably feel this way due to my start in life.

My first operation was at the tender age of two days old! The doctors cut from my tail bone to the pubic bone, then from the pubic line up to just under my ribs. And, I was only 4 lbs, so was like being cut in half.

Doctors had to be convinced to operate on me, thank God for a persuasive mother and father. No doubt everyone around me was concerned, and here it is, here is my unique story, and until now my private journey. Over my sixty-three years, my twenty-two operations and procedures still have me alive and kicking.

When those amazing surgeons cut me in half at two days old, pulled the bowel down, and re-hooked up the urethra, they basically created an entirely new map of my system. Despite this birth defect my parents taught me to believe I was fairly normal.

Travel with me through my struggles and funny experiences I encountered along the way. Hopefully, I can inspire others to navigate their medical challenges in a positive forward direction. Also learn how my personal story of my faith, family, love for sport and *sense of humour* piggy-backed me through my daily health struggles.

Wow, I Chose to Live Life

My father read a draft of this book, and said "Why haven't you put something in the book about your accomplishments?" Quite frankly I had not really thought about adding that to my story. I look at the opportunities that came my way as just that; gifts to not waste. But you know what, I have earned and worked hard to move forward and contribute to society.

The world doesn't revolve around me, but I think it knows I'm here. I had some great plans and dreams of what I could do professionally, who I would marry, and what my life would be like. Can the 'I wants' develop into 'I can'? These are the questions I had to ask myself growing up with a hidden handicap. The statement needed to be 'I want to' or "Oh yes, I can." Like my father, I asked myself what tools do I have to use. What are my capabilities, training, and experience on which to build? How do I appear to others? Do they think me capable, smart and experienced enough? Do they respect my work effort and people skills?

Just like others, I was given a set of talents, a level of intelligence and capabilities to balance along with my physical limitations. I also believe my physical challenges taught me how to generate will power, how to get up when I was down. Every single night while I lie on the floor in pain, and need to get up to continue my medical procedure 'enema', I have taught myself to "just to do it, to persevere." I really do not have a choice. Is that an accomplishment? I would say, "yes".

I have noticed forgetfulness, and difficulty following along, and staying on task during department meetings. I would catch myself asking a question that was just discussed, a very embarrassing moment when these situations occurred. I am after all getting older.

I have had flash backs of my continued struggle academically through school. I failed math, English, French, chemistry, etc., but for some reason I was still interested in these subjects. I remember sitting in my desk fighting back the tears, and at times, wondering what I will do in life. I may have been the worst student in my high school. However, I definitely tried as hard as possible to understand, and learn the logarithms, French verbs and English grammar. When I look back, I know I had learning challenges, likely a result of the numerous fevers, medications and anesthesia over the years.

Small Successes

Luckily for me I had my singing voice, and was a very good skier. What we enjoy, we remember easily. These two skills carried me through my high school trials. They were activities where I excelled. The success of these two activities introduced what it felt like to have self-confidence.

As I grew and developed physically related medical issues were readdressed time after time. The impact these ailments had on me are addressed throughout the book at different times in my life. It's been a challenge, and necessary for me to joke with nurses, doctors, or orderlies who would escort me to surgery. I noticed laughter would lighten up the mood and distract my fear. I also would pray along with my parents and family. It was my quest to find humour with anyone that came in to poke, prod or give and take from me. I wanted to feel their smile: it made me feel better, and it gave me courage.

I come across as confident and energetic, it's my way of visualizing life. I have practiced my whole life to cover up my health, yes, digging down deep and physically acting like I am feeling fantastic. I have become that strong happy woman because I decided there was no other choice, but to take what God gave me with a sense of humour and move forward.

A Special Message!

If I were to die today, I would have to say "Well, that is not a good thing, but I have lived life!"

I love to dance. If I had one wish before I die it would be to go dancing and singing at the top of my lungs. I feel so close to God when on a run, iPod blasting. I sing and perform some of my special dance moves….please, let me go that way.

Some say I am blessed with natural rhythm, I just can't sit still when a good piece of music comes on. I will dance with total strangers, if the mood is right. I feel the music deep in my soul and it makes me feel amazing. I don't understand why all of us aren't blessed with this love for music. After all we have movement that is rhythmical that has been going on since before we were born. Our heart beats diastolic, systolic, diastolic, stronger, weaker, stronger, weaker, ba boom, pause ba boom, pause. Believe it, I take my pulse every night before sleep and after my daily medical procedure. It calms me, as I concentrate on slow breathing. At times I will play soothing music on my iPod, slowly tapping my foot to relax. Yes, music therapy is medicinal.

It's important for me to take deep breaths, holding each one, taking in more air, then slowly exhale. I repeat this in the bathroom during my daily medical procedure to handle the bloating and pressure. I visualize a special place in my life…Second Gap! A beautiful stretch of beach on the Sunshine Coast of British Columbia. I can feel the warm white sand between my toes, eagles and seabirds singing and gracefully playing in the wind, and the quiet calm breeze in my face. Everyone under stress should have a special place to retreat to in their mind and soul when they close their eyes.

It is the time in my life where I am coming to terms with physical deterioration, aging, and I don't mind saying, this is a frustrating reality. I am now cautious in order to be able to continue to take care of my health, do 'my thing', and enjoy the balance of my life. I am excited about the inspiration received from a simple decision to make an effort to accept self-help and to dedicate myself to further learning.

A Gift I Cherish

I picture myself standing at the top of a snow blown cornice, bright sunshine; the snow is absolutely perfect. As I glance over the edge and shift my weight, the snow crunches and squeaks beneath my skis. It's steep, I love the rush, and am not one to take the easy road. I can't give in to a bad edge, and must be prepared to fight my way out of a fall. My heart races, but I'm at peace, confident I have the skill and knowledge to ski the steep powder terrain, all the while knowing I will show the hill whose boss. "I am awesome!"

My heels lift, and I sail off the edge of the cornice, ready to touch down in the narrow chute. Landing softly, the light powder explodes under my feet, and up over my torso, blinding me momentarily. Instinctively I set my pole, simultaneously driving my knees into the hill. I sink and prepare to reload, shoulders facing square to the fall line, as I carve the next turn leaving my crystal tracks in the snow behind me. I have the feeling of flight. I am in heaven, in total control. I am alive! I have just experienced one of God's heaven on earth experiences. And I can do it again, and I know I will. I am empowered!

"God, thank you for my journey, and 'Yes', I include all the operations and stuff I have been forced to navigate through daily. I know that when I was born, you, God, looked down on me and said, 'Ah, I will let this little one live'.

Having conflicting thoughts all of my life regarding my body, I would tell people, "I am thinking about writing a book." Of course they would ask, "What is it about? I sometimes paused and wondered if I could trust them with this information. I wondered if they would make fun of me or think, "Oh my, she just talked about her bowels." At first, I simply talked about how it is private, or just multiple operations.

Little by little people were allowed in on my journey, and my story. I have said to my husband, "I don't think I can do this." All of the information is so very private. I don't want to embarrass my family. This experience of writing a book has been eye opening. However, I could not keep my secret, my hidden handicap quiet any longer. I need for the public to know the sacrifices my parents, husband, children, and friends have made for me. It is so very liberating to see and hear reactions to my stories. I hope people will learn from this. After all, "There is a lot to learn in this world, and the sun is setting."

One of the most proud times of my life are when my children step up and check in on each other, and give fabulous advice and support when needed. I love how they communicate with their father. He has been my back bone for 44 fabulous years. I owe my family everything. As important, my parents, I owe them my life, especially Mom. I could die smiling, knowing my parents' are so very proud of me, our family, my accomplishments and of whom I have become.

I gain strength, happiness and feel good volunteering my time to young people who need help, or advising a client how to find that their life really can be in their control.

In my quest to really live, I learned about some of my limitations and strengths. I just wanted to live life and at times, took on the challenges of travel and sports to attempt and succeed at just that 'living'.

What Do I Have To Complain About?

Pay it forward and reach out to others who may benefit in some small way.

My youngest asked if his father and I would join him, along with a few others at the 2012 CFL All-Stars in a visit to the "sick kids" Children's Hospital while visiting in Toronto during the 100th CFL Grey Cup celebrations. Entering the hospital, walking down the hall, it surprised me how suddenly I flashed back and faced memories of fear, and needed to go off by myself to gather my wits. The pads on the bumper handrails for wheelchairs, the children's cartoon painting along the walls, and, wow, I was back in a darker place again.

The smoke stack outside the windows, reminded me of the one I stared at when stuck in bed with tubes attached to so many places. I recalled how I was forced to maneuver just to roll over in order to avoid bending IV tubes, an adjustment to prevent those lovely bed sores. Why it is the sheets in the hospitals were so rough anyway?

Sitting at the windows at Vancouver General I would watch for a visitor, wanting conversation. I would watch the cars drive by making up stories of where they were headed. I felt imprisoned and was looking for some resemblance of a normal kids life. I was often reminded of my plight when doctors would say, "You may be going home soon."

No specific date or time, "Just soon." Then, the next news, "Well you need another operation; you may be here for a few more weeks."

Mostly being in the Toronto Children's Hospital reminded me of the scared thoughts that had consumed me daily.

Now a mother, I was amazed at how real the fear is for all of the parents we met that day. We were introduced to children with very serious issues, and their parents who didn't know what the outcome would be for their baby. Their eyes told of their pain. These families were separated from one another. They had to rearrange careers, organize other family members, find places to live and try to find some normalcy in these dark and uncertain times.

It was painful to re-live this once again. I walked out of the hospital convinced to volunteer, to 'pay it forward', to help the parents and staff who need a break from the daily fight, not knowing what their future holds. It is a simple thing to do. I want to help them with a smile.

I am grateful for prayer, and will never give up on the power of prayer. The people I met spoke of it and believe. They spoke of faith and hope. I get it!

I will leave you with one of my favorite sayings: *'It is not our abilities that show who we are, it is our choices.'* I chose to let people into my world. I thank God once again for a sense of humour.

Yes, how we handle life's challenges is a choice. When life throws a curve ball, and it results in a strike against us, hit the next one out of the park and experience the joy.

Mary Anne Patricia Catherine O'leary

It all started with a very happy young handsome couple who married at the end of WW II. Unknowingly they were to face terrifying challenges forcing them to embrace their strength and faith in order to provide and live as normal a family life as possible.

My Dad worked for a large corporation in the paper industry. In 1946 my older brother was born in Los Angeles, and in 1948 my father was transferred to Davenport, Iowa with family in tow.

A year later Mom was pregnant and read an article in the newspaper about twins, and said to my Dad, "Wouldn't it be great to have twins? But that won't happen as we don't have a history of twins in our families."

1950

Early on Mom started to retain fluid. Her belly became so large she had to stop driving the car as she couldn't get the seat back far enough. Her whole body was swollen from her hands to her toes, so her doctor ordered her to stay in bed for the rest of her pregnancy. The doctor told her that to save her life they would have to induce labor which was created greater risk for the baby as well. Either way there was concern. This, of course, meant the baby would be premature.

Once induced she was off to the delivery room to have what she thought would be one baby. She and my father had no clue what was going to be their fate with the new addition, or should I add multiples. As it turned out, I was born at 4lbs 3 ounces, and Catherine was born at 4 lbs 4 ounces, five minutes apart.

Mom still had to care for my rambunctious four year old brother. Like any expecting parent, she prepared for one new born. The doctors didn't want my mother to get over excited. She has noted her doctor withheld his twin suspicions so she wouldn't worry. Surprise, Mom and Dad now had three children: a four year old, and two tiny premature twin girls.

Immediately after 'We' were born, the doctors told Dad there were some very serious issues with Baby A, me. Dad relayed the information to Mom, but played it down a bit. The next day the doctor had to tell Mom that Baby A would most certainly die due to her intestinal disorders, as I was born without any exits.

In this Catholic Mercy Hospital, the nuns were told of my condition, so they rushed me off and baptized me, giving me the name of Mary. I wonder if they called baby boys Jesus or Thomas, something Christian.

It is important to note that while all of this was happening, my Dad's cousin, Mimi took care of my older brother. He was left with whoever could take him for this time. This must have been an added stress for my parents. Daily life with family is challenging at best, however, when you add these worries, my parents had to do whatever it took. They did well.

I was born with multiple congenital anomalies, including a partial bowel, double vagina, double uterus, partially dysfunctional kidney and blocked urethras. The bottom half of these organs were as I understood it throughout my whole life at birth as stump of thick fat. Yet, on a positive note I did have ovaries, two uteri as well!

Doctors informed my parents they had never previously experienced a newborn patient with these types of anomalies.

They said, "Even if we were to try to do something, the baby won't survive being out of the incubator for that length of time. Please prepare yourselves. Adding, "Would you like to hold Baby A or not?"

I cannot imagine what an emotional impact this must have had on this young couple, my Mom and Dad in their twenties. My parents chose to hold me, and said "Hail Mary's" over me. Mom recently told me that she really didn't want to give me back to the doctors. Being strong of faith, and wanting the doctors to see what they could do, Mom and Dad pressed the doctors to try, try, and please try to save me.

The doctors must have thought and studied and spoke to other specialists. Despite the poor prognosis, the doctors preceded this ground breaking procedure. A standard procedure in the medical community in the 40's and 50's was to just 'set infants aside' with serious medical conditions to die.

Yeah! Thanks, Mom and Dad for doing that, thanks for being my voice!

Mercy Hospital Nov. 4 1950

The surgeons were not sure what to expect when they opened me up, but thankfully this first stage of a very long series of operations were successful. Thank you, well done doctors!

This is how I understand it. Doctor's reports are enclosed with medical terms.

My first operation was when I was two days old. I was born with an imperforated anus and blind ending rectal pouch. I needed construction of a rectum as well as an anal orifice. Given my small size exploratory probing was not possible as the additional anomalies and conditions were not fully recognizable. The doctors were able to open my bowel by pulling my rectum pouch down in order to create an anus.

Surgery completed, and the surgeons announced they doubted my survival and told my parents as much. As they had to recreate and construct a lower gastrointestinal and urinary opening, I lacked the normal defecatory musculature and sphincters, thus I would have to give myself enemas for the rest of my life—once I was old enough. In my first seven years it was Mom's job to perform the enema procedure.

Mom was willing to do anything to physically care for me, and Dad was acutely aware from what the doctors had warned, the medical bills will be high. In 1950, his company didn't have medical insurance for staff's children.

My First operation - Medical Report

November 4, 1950
Mercy Hospital
Dr. Brown and Wm. Brown

Incision of imperforated anus – construction of rectum, plastic repair of imperforated anus.

Under general anesthesia by Dr. Herath, patient was placed in lithotomy position. Perineum was scrubbed with soap and water and painted with tincture of Merthiolate. Incision was made from the posterior aspect of the genitalia to the coccyx through the midline, splitting the sphincter in two halves. Hemostasis was secured by ligating bleeding points with 000 plain c.g. Dissection of the perimeum continued inward through the fat to expose the blind end of the rectal pouch. This blind end of rectal pouch was caught with thumb forceps and gentle traction was made upon it, while blunt dissection with the finger or an instrument having a piece of cotton was used to separate the tissues at the cleavage line. In dissecting the rectal pouch from the sacral area this was readily done without any difficulty. However, in dissecting the rectal pouch from the vagina it was noted at the upper end of the vagina that where separation of the rectum occurred, there developed a hole in the posterior wall of the vagina. There was no leakage of urine or meconium at this time. This hole in the posterior aspect of the vagina allowed the smallest size catheter to pass. However, in spite of this hole, dissection of the rectal pouch continued until all structures attached to it were separated, and the pouch could be brought down to the

11

skin edge of the perineum. This was accomplished. It was noted that the rectal pouch was open when it was brought down into view and ready to be opened for suturing. The pouch appeared to be open on the end. It was felt that this open end of the rectal pouch represented the fistulous tract which was probably not opened into the vagina. Because of the plugging there was no meconium allowed to pass through the vaginal track. No attempt was made to suture the hole in the posterior aspect of the vagina because of the minuteness of the tissues here and the difficulty in visualization of structures. The blind end of the rectal pouch which was now opened was sutured to the edges of the skin after the sphincter muscle was sutured as accurately as possible. On either side of the new anal opening which was placed approximately between the two halves of the anal sphincter the skin was sewed with interrupted 000 black silk. The mucus membrane of the rectal pouch and the skin were sutured together with interrupted 000 chromic g.g. After completion of this suture line was fairly accurately approximated, and would be relatively waterproof. Some irrigation of the colon, which was now brought down to fashion a new anus, was irrigated with a 5 cc. syringe and some thick, sticky gelatinous meconium was removed from this portion of the rectum. Extensive probing was not done. The patient apparently withstood the operation procedure fairly well, and also withstood the anesthesia fairly well, and was sent back to its room in good condition.

FINDINGS: A blind surgical pouch, was, as x-ray study indicated, about 2 ½ cm. above the anal dimple of the perineum. It is believed that this anal pouch was attached to the posterior aspect of the upper vaginal tract by a fistulous tract which was not opened, but this was opened inadvertently while separating the rectal pouch from the posterior wall of the vagina.

At the time of the dissection there was no mecomium that was demonstrated in the vagina and very little of it appeared at the new anal opening after this was completed. The explanation of this lack of the appearance of mecomium is probably easily explained on the basis of material being very thick, sticky, and gelatinous. A curved Rochester pin clamped and inserted into the segment of the bowel that was brought down to fashion the new anus, yielded some of this thick, gelatinous meconium. There was no evidence of other anomalies at the time of this dissection procedure, though it was impossible to say whether or not there were G.I. anomalies beyond the vision of the surgeon. These may be suspected however.

End of Report

When my parents were told I had survived the surgery they must have been so very relieved and probably cried, 'Thanks to God'. Again and again in those early days of life, my parents were warned to prepare themselves for my little body's malfunction, to virtual self-destruction.

When they announced this to my older brother, he added, "This is my little sister! We need to give her a middle name!"

So they added 'Anne'. My parents wanted an Irish name, hence I was baptized 'Patricia'. I know this name game is so very complicated. But, it is what it is, Mary Anne Patricia. All my life, except when my mother called knowing I had done something wrong, I have been called Patty. To this day the whole thing is confusing. When I hit a bad shot in tennis or golf I refer to myself as "Oh Mary Anne!"

Mom and Dad were, of course, thinking of other worries than problems choosing a name, and had to just keep putting one foot in front of the other, day by day, *"Will baby "A" live today?"*

At that time, they also had two other children to take care of. They needed to worry about who was going to take care of Danny and how my incubated premature twin, Catherine was doing.

So this was the start of my journey, and at times the many scary questions that drifted through my brain? What can I do to make the pain go away? Will I live? What kind of life will I have? And yet, I will add, oh my gosh, I am so very blessed to be alive story. People have been so very kind when they have said to me, "You are so brave."

I usually think or respond, "What choice do I have?" The brave for me are the doctors, medical staff, and my parents who dealt with the everyday responsibilities of care when faced with my survival and dignity.

Fortunately the specialists kept their eye on my long term outcome. They created a foundation from which future surgery would continue to adjust my system in order for me to have an active, relatively healthy life. Their early vision of my future was a series of surgical building blocks. My doctors reached out to other specialists in order to find ways for me to have as much of a normal life as possible.

Numerous times over the course of my life doctors have said, "Are you aware of how complicated your system is?"

What I get most of the time, "You are functioning with what you have, so keep going."

A specialist recently told me, "You have the better of two bad situations. At least, you are not wearing a sack (colostomy) on the outside for your bowel drainage."

I know that I'm not alone; there are countless others with hidden handicaps who feel trapped in their own bodies. We can't always change what we were born with. Not everyone is able to live with normal bodily functions. We must accept and decide to do what we can with what we have. We must go deep into ourselves and find that hidden strength that is there, we just need to look for it, then go out and create a new path!

I want you to know how much the many who are handicapped need love, support, understanding and our patience. I find myself a few times a week saying out loud, "What do I have to complain about?"

After my initial surgery, Mom was to stay in bed for a week. I bet that did not really suit her well. She is a fire cracker, so was probably moving up and down the stairs to check on her new baby girls. While in the hospital, Mom would sleep in a cot next to me. Catherine as a premature infant was doing well in the baby ward, while I was in the high risk baby area. We were both in incubators, so we couldn't be together. A few months ago, I did ask my mother, "Mom, didn't you have any good times with Cathy?" She stated, "I was glad to have twins, but too busy and stressed to say it was enjoyable."

She explained the two baby girls were on two different formulas. Then she made a third formula to try to get both of us to take in order that she would not have to make two different formulas daily. She said it was a challenge to keep up with the feedings, diaper changes, and my enema, etc. She had us both in the same crib, one on each end.

She hired a diaper service which delivered clean ones and also picked up the soiled diapers. Still all cloth diapers with pins, etc. She was busy with taking care of a four year old and two premature babies, while Dad was off to Atlanta on his work transfer. My parents were encouraged with each transfer, as along with the move came a promotion, and a bump in salary.

My great grandfather, on Mom's side, John Collins who had also lost a baby infant, sent a rocking chair to Mom. Mom said she would rock us, one at a time. Still to this day, she has that rocker, and all of my siblings, all her grandchildren, and now her great grandbaby have been rocked in that chair that arrived in the mail. 'Great gift, Great Grandpa, thanks.'

After my initial surgery, Mom's time was filled up taking me back and forth to the hospital, and figuring out how to function as our new family of five.

The stress on my father must have been horrendous. Not really knowing how many surgeries I may need must have been an extra motivation to go out and sell, sell and sell more of the paper products. I can only imagine the worry he must have had while traveling between small mid-western towns for weeks at a time, wondering what was going on at home.

Soon after our birth and the initial surgery, my grandmother arrived by train from Los Angeles to Davenport, Iowa, to help my parents. As we, Catherine and I were premature, no one from either side of the family was able to be on hand to help on November 2, 1950.

Mom has never referred to this time as wonderful, as she and Dad never were able to celebrate this miracle. Twins, wow! No baby showers, no parties. They had to work at keeping strong day to day with their worry about me.

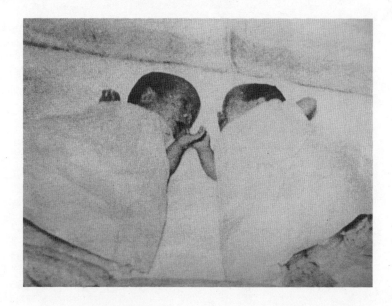

The Only Picture of Cathy and I Together.

This was likely a very happy time for our young family. The miracle of birth, and our amazing surgeons had our family growing, and my family feeling quite good.

When the doctors thought I was strong enough, my parents brought the two of us home, and then my Grandmother returned to Los Angeles.

A Twinless Twin

Then, as Mom describes *"The Week from Hell"* consumed our family.

Monday January 22ⁿᵈ 1951, Dad receives a phone call, and is transferred to Atlanta, Georgia. He leaves Davenport for Atlanta immediately for meetings.

Tuesday January 23ʳᵈ, My Mom bought train tickets to take us to Atlanta, to meet up with Dad. Catherine started to make stressed breathing noises.

Wednesday January 24th, preparations for the move. Mom tried to burp her, and then there was silence. She called a neighbor who is a fireman. The ambulance is called, and my little sister in less than five minutes passes away. In comments to me years later, Mom very quietly added, "You have no idea how that silence sounds."

Friday January 26th, funeral preparation (I assume, Mom and Dad left this one blank – I would, too.)

Saturday January 27ᵗʰ, funeral

Sunday January 28ᵗʰ, Friends came down to check on us, as our family was so very far away.

Tuesday January 29ᵗʰ, Dad left again to start his new position in Atlanta.

Wednesday January 30ᵗʰ, Mother left with my brother and me for the train. She said, "I had to figure out how to give you enemas on the train."

Letter written on January 28ᵗʰ, Norwalk, California, by my Great Auntie Helen

Dear Nadine and George,

I cannot tell you how sad I was when Mother phoned me regarding little Cathy's death.

I know it must have been a terrible shock to you both, but I know you will accept this in a truly religious spirit; it surely must have been the Lord's will.

As for little Cathy she will be happy in heaven and will be spared all the trials of this life. I know it isn't easy to look upon this in this way just now, but know you will be brave for Danny's sake.

I am so happy to hear that you are coming out here for a while Nadine, a change will be good for you and Danny, and Patti will enjoy it too. I wish George could come along too but perhaps that is not possible just now.

I want to congratulate you George on your fine promotion. I think you will all enjoy Atlanta; from what all the southerners I have met say about Georgia it must be a delightful spot.

Will make this short this time my dears- I just wanted you to know that I am thinking of you very often these days.

Love and kisses, Auntie Helen

Still, even at 63 years I feel a strong pull from my twin sister. I know for a fact she is looking down on me and is thrilled I have survived all the surgeries and chose to live a positive life.

The studies I've read on 'twinless twins' feel, although I find it difficult to believe, the mothers of surviving twins don't have time to mourn, are over-protective, and expect more than usual from the surviving twin. Many twins that survive depend on each other as best friends for everything. Other twins have opposite personalities, are idealized, competitive and/or are prone to sibling attachment identity. I really don't know what kind of relationship Catherine and I would have had together; this has always been an obvious curiosity for me.

I am a monozygotic "identical" twinless twin. Yes, I am sober when I just wrote that. Identical twins start as the same zygote (egg) and about 8 days after fertilization, this egg splits to two embryos. Dizygotic (fraternal) twins are two separate eggs fertilized by two sperm.

A single birth is called singleton, and a general term for offspring of a multiple birth is multiple.

Due to limited size of the womb, multiple pregnancies are much less likely to carry full term than single births. Twin births typically are carried to 37 weeks (3 weeks less than full term) on average.

The people who live in Yoruba have the highest twinning births in the world, 90 to 100 per 1000 births. This is possibly because of high consumption of a specific type of YAM containing a natural phytoestrogen which may stimulate ovaries to release an egg from each side. Women who have a family history of fraternal twins have a higher chance of producing fraternal twins themselves, as there is a genetically linked tendency to hyper-ovulate. There is no known link for identical twinnings. Other factors that increase odds of fraternal twins include maternal age, fertility drugs or treatments.

Very few understand the twin bond, and even fewer understand the loss of the twin bond. I found little research on 'twinless twins'. For that matter, there isn't much on what siblings go through either. Generally speaking the worst bereavement is spousal or child loss. Twin bereavement is given a lot of attention in many tribal cultures throughout the world.

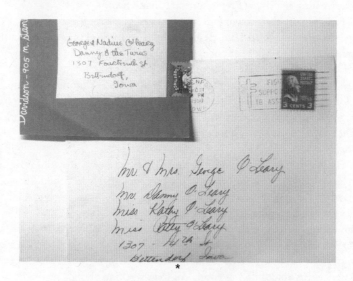

"Danny and the Twins", "Miss Kathy O'Leary"

At the time of Cathy's death, I was too young, to have any memory of the brief time she was alive. As I got older, some of the typical grief symptoms occurred, guilt (lots and lots of that), sleeplessness, depression, anger, shock and confusion.

My older brother knew something was going on, as the ambulance took Catherine away. According to Mom, he was really courageous and supportive. Being only four years old, he never complained.

There are, of course, my reactions to my twin's absence when I was in adolescence and as an adult. I admit that there are many times having looked into the mirror, wondering if I were looking at my twin, is this what it would feel like?

I have had short conversations in the mirror, telling her that I am sorry she is not here. I feel guilty I survived. She would probably be the smart one. I have asked her what she thinks of my husband and our family? I know this may sound odd, but at times I sense she's looking back at me.

I had less than three months with her. If you notice in the photo, we are holding hands, eyes wide open and smiling at each other. That says it all. I have wondered if she had survived, "Would she also have had similar medical problems?"

Last year I was discussing the loss of my twin with a doctor friend, and he said something to me so very profound, "So, you had two uteri, two vaginas. Maybe there was another baby?"

When my friend asked about the autopsy, I said, "Well I found out they did discover my twin had an oversized heart."

As far as triplets, we will never really know.

Here is an odd reaction: When I meet someone that either speaks of twins or is a twin, I used to say "I was a twin." Then not long ago I would say "I am a twin, but lost her at a very young age." Now I reply, "*I am a twinless twin.*"

That really says it all. Growing up I was treated like a singleton. That was confusing to my identity. I am what I am. Being a twin is an integral part of my identity. It is amazing how I want to talk about her.

I miss her! "Is that possible?" It happens all of the time!

On my birthdays we never mentioned Cathy unless I brought her up. I have noticed for my whole life that my parents in conversation would state they had four children, when in actual fact they had five. I may add since I started writing this book my mother says she had five, understandably, they didn't want to re-open the pain or memory.

As a family that moved around, we created a picture of a happy healthy family. I am certain my parents did not bring up the fact they had lost a child. In those days there were not the type of services and counseling for my parents, my older brother and me as are readily available in today's society.

As time went by and because of my parent's strength, faith and sense of humour, we did have some great fun times. Even to this day, we do 'hang out' and are extremely close. My parents did have other children and my younger brother and sister didn't seem to notice this void. Life was good. We were working on moving on; finding life's joys to piggy-back us through the tough times.

We Meet Once Again!

Ever since I can remember I have not really felt I was a good twin sister. I wanted to go and visit her gravesite, but it's half way across the country, and I was anxious about how I might handle such a visit. My parents had really not spoken about how beautiful Iowa is, likely it recalled sad memories.

My dear husband had taken a business trip in the area in 1995, and made a point to locate and visit her grave site. He took pictures of the grave stone, and I remember staring at the photo. Wow, it must be true!

My parents, my older brother and I moved to Georgia the week after her death. For many years I felt guilty, as she was not always on my mind. I learned later, much later as an adult that my Dad would send flowers on our birthday. There was no way of knowing if the flowers ever made it to the grave site, no photo, just blind faith that it happened.

In the summer of 2006 with our children old enough to be on their own, my husband asked if I would like to accompany him on a business trip across the country. I would be able to visit my sister's gravesite! I was excited, but extremely scared, too.

Off we went, driving through the northwestern states, headed for the mid-west United States. I was amazed and thrilled at the beauty and vastness of the landscape. We travelled through Idaho and Nevada endless miles of high plains with wild burros, antelope, and deer, into Colorado and Wyoming, Nebraska, then finally my birth state of Iowa.

As we approached Iowa, I was feeling very anxious. My parents had given instructions on whom to look up and that we were searching for the only Catholic cemetery in Davenport, and of course reminding us, at the time, Catherine passed away 56 years ago!

I had also told Greg, "When we find the grave, please leave me alone. Please get far away from me." I had penned up grieving and emotion, and I needed to be alone with just Catherine.

We were traveling along the freeway, when suddenly there was the sign, 'Welcome to Iowa'. I started taking pictures of the very cool corn fields that were terraced against the blue sky. It was absolutely beautiful. My little sister was making my visit welcoming and heartwarming.

We pulled off to ask directions, and I phoned my parents who were waiting in anticipation from home. They too were thrilled we had arrived in Iowa.

We drove towards the area and found the great Mississippi River. We crossed the bridge, and I was just soaking it all in while my husband kept driving to where the people had directed us to go.

We had to find "the only Catholic Cemetery". The directions were for us to walk into the entrance, office on the left, and turn left to look for Catherine's gravesite along side the road. This was supposed to be the newborn section.

My heart pumping we pulled into a gorgeous cemetery with huge monuments and mature trees. The entire area was well kept, and I was speechless. I was finally going to see my sister. Could this be real, did I really have a sister, a twin? I needed proof.

We started to walk into the gate. We could not see the Catholic Cemetery sign, but we had followed instructions. Also my husband said that it looked just like the place he visited a few years back.

We went through the gates, but there was no office, so we started to look for the grave turning left up the road. The place was huge. There were no maps of the plots and no way to find anyone among the many historical statues and family plots that dated back to 1690's.

Finally we came upon the newborn area. We walked around and around reading the face of each gravestone, but with no luck. I was really upset. What is going on? The cemetery covered acres, and we had covered a very good chunk of it, crossing back and forth in grids. It was starting to get dark. "Did we come all this way not find her?"

It takes a Sense of Humour!

I kept telling myself, "Fine, at least she's in a gorgeous place." We had to give up our search, we left the cemetery for our hotel. My husband was dumbfounded. Luckily he had taken the pictures from his previous visit, so I had some record of her resting place.

I was in shock, "What just happened?" This was not fair. I had to phone my parents. The extreme disappointment in their voices was loud and clear. Devastated, we drove back to the hotel. We pulled into the hotel, and Greg went to check in. As I sat there very sad and staring out the car window, I noticed all the license plates said Illinois. Every one of the plates were Illinois, Illinois!

I raced into the hotel and asked, "Are we in Illinois?" "Of course!" the attendant replied.

Greg and I looked at each other and smiled. But he had appointments a state away the next day. There would not be time for us to go back over the bridge and the Mississippi River to the state to Iowa and look for Catherine again. I don't mind saying I was very, very upset, we were having to leave, without ever seeing her grave site.

Twin Sister Trickery

We awoke to an overcast day, which didn't help my mood. We climbed into the truck and Greg turned the key, but the engine was a dead as a door nail, yes, it would not start.

Suddenly this man appeared from out of nowhere. He startled the both of us. "Hi, it looks like your truck needs repair. There's a garage just down the road." We called the garage and they agreed to tow the truck to their shop to check it out. A few hours later they announced we would have to get a part delivered, and we could have the truck up and running by the next morning.

We would have to stay for another day! Hey, I think my little angel was there to make certain we stayed around. We got a loaner car and were chuckling. My husband knew what this meant and was thrilled at our situation. This could have happened in Washington, Oregon, Nevada, Colorado, Wyoming or Nebraska or when we went through Iowa, but it happened now. Yes, this was very convenient. Who broke the truck? Back in the hotel room sitting in silence, thinking the same thoughts, Hmmm, I wonder, "Thank you Cathy!"

So Greg made a few changes to the meeting schedule, and he said, "Let's go look for Catherine in 'Iowa' !"

We decided to look up my Dad's cousin. She was a bit younger than my parents, and had taken care of my brother when my Mom went into the hospital in 1950. When she answered the phone, she yelled in shock and emotion,

"It's the twin, it's the twin, and she's alive!"

"I was what?" I thought to myself, what she meant was I am alive, of course I am. Her reaction reminded me that when we left Iowa in 1951 the doctors had warned everyone I would probably not survive. That was a very weird reminder. Of course, these relatives hadn't heard anything about how I was doing, ever. They just assumed after our move that I didn't make it.

This was a huge gift. Wow, someone knew us back then. Someone else knew my twin. I really had a twin sister. Oh my gosh!

We visited my relatives that evening. They really didn't have much to add to my saga. The older relatives had all passed away. Carmelita (Mimi) had a few memories, and after we told her our previous exploits across the river in Illinois, she pointed out that, "The only 'Catholic' cemetery in Davenport was just a half a mile away, "It's just down the road!"

Try Try Again

Bright and early the next morning; we were off again to look for my twin sister, Catherine. We drove back 'across the Mississippi', this time from Illinois where our hotel was into 'Iowa', through the old town of Davenport, and found the only Catholic cemetery.

Once again I felt great anxiety, my heart pounding. True enough, we parked and walked through the old gates, and there on our left was the office. After flipping through some old records, the attendant told us the children's grave site was literally outside the door, up the road on our left. That's all I needed to hear.

Her Gravesite

There on the ground was a small loose stone, about 12"long x 8"wide x 6" thick in size. The grave stone simply read:

"CATHERINE O'LEARY Nov. 2, 1950 - Jan. 25, 1951"

When I saw the date, I broke down saying"She has the same birthday as I do!" I repeated this three times."Look she's an O'Leary!" my family surname. I lost it, for thirty minutes or more. We, Irish really know how to wail. This moment and the reality of finally seeing the grave hit me so very hard (*note-even when I edit this…I have tears).

The note I had written to her, several years before at the time of my husband's last visit was still in the plastic bag beneath the grave stone. The baggy was warn with holes, likely due to the stone being knocked time and time again by the grass mower. I removed the note and read it out loud to my little sister.

I was glad to be alone with Cathy. Here we are,"The O'Leary twins together at last, in spirit." This is real!"We would have been a force to reckon with!"

When I calmed down Greg came over, saying some sweet words to her about me and our great family.

August 23, 2004, 54 years and 235 days later we meet once again!

Before we left I placed a little angel statue next to her. I told her "Little sister, I am going to live my life learning and laughing in your honor" I added, "OK, but I won't see you in heaven for awhile, I have a lot of living to do for the two of us, I love you!"

And I know she responded in true O'Leary humour, "You better!"

The magnitude of what my parents must have felt to leave their child hit me like nothing I have ever felt. My Mom, days after Catherine passed, boarded the train with my older brother and me, and left her three month old baby.

I kept saying to Greg, "I can't leave her, I can't. Not again!" I now knew I had a sister! My twin, Catherine!

Later that day, I phoned my parents once my emotions were reconciled, told them of the funny search, and mentioned she is well looked after. Across the little path that winds through the cemetery is a plot for an O'Leary clan. She is never really alone, she is in good company, and we all keep her in our thoughts.

We continued our trip, crossed the Mississippi River again, and soon arrived back in Illinois. A storm, like we had never seen before hit, and forced Greg to pull off the road. Rain, wind, hale and lightning were all around us. I think my twin was sending a message, "Can't you stay a little longer; can't we have more visits?"

This is another time I am grateful for my faith. I know she is looking out for me. I do believe she is the reason I am still on this side of the grass, I am alive for both of us!

My father always said, "Can you imagine two of you on this earth? That would have been awesome!" It would have been something, a huge challenge just for people to get a word in edgewise, lots of laughter, and she probably would have been taller than I am, or…She would have been…Just like Me!

Many times I have looked in the mirror, I see her, and yes, I even say out loud, "Hi Cathy, I love you!"

It is not news to see how much of a void this was in my life, being a twinless twin. Questions came up like, "Why did I feel a need to have a Best Friend?" "Why when I was young did I leave a space next to me on my desk bench for my guardian angel?", "Why did I have such jealousy when I would meet or see twins?" I still do have these thoughts even at my older age.

When I look in the mirror, at times I see my twin; and she winks at me, and she adds, "Ok, go out there and live life for the both of us today, you *Rock!*"

Jumping Forward to Dec. 26th 2012

It is wonderful I found this surprise package. I had a chance to mourn a little more, this time with my parents. Once again, this treasure was more proof that this was really my history.

Christmas 2012 was over, my husband and I are staying a few days with my parents who were nearly ninety years of age to help clean up after our celebrations. The kitchen is cleaned up, and most of the clan had gone home. Dec. 26th is "Boxing Day", and the family is relaxing. My younger brother was taking down the tree, Dad was in the living room working on his book. Mother was no doubt touching up in the kitchen, and my husband was in the family room editing this book. I decided to go through my parent's very old memorabilia chest to see if I could find any photos for both this and for my father's book.

After two hours, I was getting tired of pulling out old heavy photo albums while at the same time fascinated by mother's and father's many accomplishments. Both my parents were on boards of directors and worked many hours for charity. Mom was a Chairman on the Board for two Vancouver hospitals. She wanted to give back to the hospitals that help young children, and she did some amazing work. My dad served on numerous hospital and business boards.

I almost forgot why I was even looking through all of this stuff. After about two or three minutes, from a pile of papers on my right an envelope slipped out. I swear it was like someone had with their finger flipped it towards me so I would notice. It distracted me away from the other photos, and I the date on it jumped out at me. It was Jan. 29 1951. I didn't think there was any information regarding that time of my life. I asked myself, "Who could this be from?" It has to be something about my twin and me, or possibly about my older brother.

As a surviving twin, it has been a challenge to not live in a sad place, but I have chosen to halt the sadness in its tracks. As I read the letter, it was Mother's best friend from Los Angeles, who was saddened, and in shock with the news of my twin's death. As I finished the letter, I found myself waling and crying, calling for my Mom and Dad. I realized they were all there for me, again.

Mother had completely forgotten about these notes, apparently she too had tried to be positive and move on, and raise the rest of her family. At the same time two small cardboard pamphlets slid off of the pile, 'all on their own'!

Ahhh, My sister is at work again. Her spirit made me notice these. Both of these were pink, white and blue and said "To Welcome The Twins". On the inside of the cover is a place to put baby's first pictures. However, there were no pictures. I believe she did this little flick to get the letters out, and I thank her for once again visiting me.

In this package of curiosity were a few more cool congratulatory cards and notes from family and new friends. It was apparent and cute that there were not many choices for twin baby cards. Two cards had the letter "S" added to baby. One person bought a card that had a baby on the cover and a different looking baby inside. She wrote a caption "the other baby" under the enclosed drawings.

Three Different Cards

Best Wishes to you and the twins

Of course, with TWINS, you'll find it's true
That you'll have TWICE as much to do—
But you'll have TWICE the joy and fun 'cause
TWO are TWICE AS CUTE AS ONE!

Some of the letters and cards asked about our weight? Asked if we had names yet? And many said, "Danny, my older brother, must be so excited and proud."

One very special letter was from Mimi. Not my grandmother, but a cousin of my father's. She is the lady that took care of my older brother when Mom and I were in the hospital, during and just after our birth.

My grandmother arrived in Iowa to be with us and BoPo (our grandfather) was not able to join her due to his work. Below is a loving letter he wrote my Mom for love and support. My Mother was very close to him. He was very kind. He lived to be 97, and my mother often spoke about the fun things they did together as well as how he taught her so very much. I would imagine my parents needed their parents at a challenging time like this. I know I certainly would. Note how he called himself her pal.

Dearest Little Sweet Heart,

Hope Mother finds you much better. Sorry I didn't write before but you know your Dad. I think of you everyday honey and wish that I could be with you with all my heart. Be careful and take good care of yourself darling, because you are very precious to me, and all of us. I would have given my anything if I could have come back with Mother. But honey, I'll be there with you in my spirit and heart every day.

I'll bet dangerous Dan sure is growing up, give him a kiss for me. I am writing this in the car on the way to the depot, will drop you a line real soon. Please keep your chin up,

Your pal and Dad, all my love and kisses!

Dad

I want to thank Catherine for aiding the discovery of this much valued information. It looks like there were some happy times with our family, you, me, our older brother and our amazing parents. "I really enjoy our short visits, We rock!"

Aren't Babies Grand!

They don't have any teeth
And they don't have much hair
They can't talk at all,
They can't walk anywhere.

They sleep all day long
And Stay up the whole night,

They yell every time,
Things don't suit 'me just right,

But with all of the worry
They cause you, by heck,
They do make a home—
(Yeh, they make it a wreck)

And they make you so happy,
So proud and so glad—
Ain't it just swell
Being Mother and Dad?

The poems and letters back then were so basic and loving. It is good to see there was some loving words and support going on.

It is a beautiful thing to see how much love our men and women give in this family. We feel each other's pain and celebrate our accomplishments; we even like to hang out with each other. We are truly blessed.

Too Young For Memories

1951 to 1956

After my first operation, and throughout infancy, my mother literally had to dilate my anus to give me enemas, to clean out my system. I weighed no more than four pounds, with fresh healing incisions and scars. How did she know how much water to put in? How did she keep it in me? It must have been very messy and excruciatingly painful for me, and stressful for Mom. She taught herself to give me enemas by laying me on my back and after putting a long surgical tube into me, she would just wait to see what came out.

Dad was transferred nearly every year from 1948 to 1956 when we moved to Vancouver, BC Canada. He traveled two to three weeks at a time. Once, while we were in Chicago, he was away for three months on a company sponsored course. He was only permitted to come home once during that entire time.

For years, my parents found themselves in a constant search for a new specialist to help me. Continually repeating my medical situation to the next doctor must have been a real frustration and nuisance. They were away from relatives, friends and any familiar support system. Dad and Mom were doing the best they could under the circumstances, and became proficient at moving, renting houses, finding new doctors. They worked hard and saved their money as I would continue to need more expensive surgeries in the near future. It taught them independence and team work.

My parents turned once again to prayer. This prayer was recently found in their chest of memorabilia, hand written by Mother on a shopping list.

Holy Ghost

Dear God, you know that I believe
Whatever you have said
But should it ever happen that

I start to doubt instead
Then, Holy Spirit strengthens me.
Take from my faults that I may see.

I have always felt it was extremely unfair for my parents, that they could not leave me. Mom was the one to give me my enemas. She couldn't take the chance of leaving me with anyone. How do you ask a babysitter to give an infant or child an enema?

Between 1951 and 1954 I was admitted to hospital numerous times, four times in Chicago alone with fecal impaction and/or cystitis. The colon was so dilated that they suspected agenesis, a not fully developed or functioning colon. My bladder did not drain properly, leading to recurrent infections. In Chicago, Dr. Barber had to catheterize me on three occasions for bladder outlet obstruction.

All during this time, my saintly Mom had to put me in cool baths to fight my constant fevers. Can you imagine a parent having to put a small baby through this? She must have gone through *hell* just following doctor's orders, trying to keep her tiny child alive.

Fortunately she learned quickly, as there was no other choice. Daily Mom had to perform a major procedure on me daily. She had to be in control, to keep me alive, never thinking about herself.

My mother's note of this time was my reported fevers were so very high no one really took her seriously. On one occasion Mom caught a nurse recording the wrong temperature on my file, when questioned, the nurse replied, "No child could have 107 F without seizures!"

Of course Mom replied with emphasis, "That's why we are here!"

I really don't have any recollections of those times. I was only a toddler, although hospital smells are reminders that continue to give me anxiety attacks. Ugh?...the smell of ether!

Numerous tests and exploratory surgery were done. But no obvious cause was found for the recurrent pyelitis kidney infections.

1954 Chicago-Operation to Clean Up Infections

The continuing kidney infections, and moturia which was treated with chemotherapy, fortunately, once again motivated the medical community to operate.

I was four years old, and my parents took me to the hospital. I vaguely recall going up some stairs and smelling a very distinctive smell. I imagine Mom and Dad were more frightened than I was, but I knew something was about to happen, once again for my health. I recall being in a bright room, people standing around with white clothes, and surgical masks covered their faces. I was lying under huge circular light- brightness everywhere and asking, "Where are my Mom and Dad?"

I was about to have surgery, what type? I didn't know. Then came the mask to my face, and the smell of ether. There is no smell like that in this world oooh-ugh, I am out.

Of course I have no memory of the operation. "What really happens to the mind and body under anesthesia is really crazy?"

Mom, Baby Patty, and Older Brother Danny

In Chicago, Dr. Potts removed a piece of tissue overlying the urethra thinking this may have caused the obstruction and recurrent attacks of pyelitis, fevers; etc. The flap of tissue was removed, resulting in near normal function!

Dear Dr. Bryans:

I shall never forget Patty O'Leary, she is one of the cutest little girls I have ever seen and also one who is having a whale of a lot of trouble. In fact, she was admitted to this hospital four times from September, 1953, to January of 1954 with two complaints of impaction of feces in the colon and /or attacks of cystitis. When she was here there was so much dilatation of the colon that we suspected agenesis of the colon.

On the first three admissions she was seen by Dr. Barber, the urologist, who, each time placed a catheter in the bladder to provide better drainage. Pyelograms were done and an intravenous pyelogram showed no change in the kidneys but enlargement of the bladder. A retropyelogram showed a little dilatation of the left kidney. Both of the pyelo-grams suggested stricture of the ureteral pelvic junction. A cystogram was done and enlargement of the bladder was found. We could never demonstrate any communication between the bowel and the bladder.

On the 4th of January, 1954, I explored the abdomen and investigated both ureteral and pelvic junctions. No abnor-mality was found. We removed a section from the recto sigmoid for microscopic examination. Dr. Barber was also at the operation. I opened the bladder and removed a piece of tissue which overhung the urethra thinking that this may have caused the obstruction and recurrent attacks of pyelitis (inflammation of the canal pelvis). Microscopic examination of the tissue removed from the colon showed a few ganglion cells. Today, I think we would interpret these ganglion cells as being normal.

We have not seen the child since her discharge January 20, 1954. I should be curious to know whether anything definite has been found as a cause of the recurrent pyelitis and,

Incidentally, give my greetings to the O'Leary's, they were such lovely people.

Sincerely, Dr. Willis J. Potts

First Memories

In this photo I am about three, and you can see pure happiness on my face.

Now as a mother, I can't imagine this little child having to undergo the daily enema procedure.

I do recall this cute outfit. Mom had me sit for what seemed hours while she painted a picture of me. She is so talented, the painting really looked like this photo.

After a few years of Mom giving me enemas, she began teaching me to squat on the toilet, at least that's what I remember. Imagine you are a young mother with two other young children (my brother Mike had arrived by now), with the worry of me and my siblings requirements daily. Add in a husband that was often away due to work..

1958 – Grade 2

I'm seven years old, and I took the bus to and from the Catholic elementary school down the hill. The bus had to stop to let the kids from the public school board. Yet again, I felt very ill, nauseous with cramps, and 'messed' my pants on the bus. The kids had a heyday with "What is that smell?" Can't honestly say I blame them.

I remember getting off of the bus and crying, trying to walk up the hill to my house. It was burning my bottom, and I was extremely uncomfortable.

These children were so very mean. *"Patty is stinky"*; *"Patty can't control her shit"*; *"Ooooh we can see the stuff!"* They threw pine cones at me and yelled to me, "This is what is in your pants." I guess that story isn't very funny.

Then the next day and for weeks after when I saw them, they would yell out *"Don't sit with her, she will stink up the bus with her s___t!"*

I was humiliated again. "Don't cry!" my mother would tell me. On this occasion I wasn't in control of my emotions. I did cry and cried a lot. I was really embarrassed, I soiled myself again. By not telling anyone, I felt in control of my destiny. I was not going to let them get to me. Yahhh, right!

Allergies

In 1958, coming home from school, I took a short cut from the bus stop to my home. I had to go through a forested area that was part of our neighbor's back yard across the street. I bumped into a tree, and before I knew it, I was surrounded by bees. I was stung just below my eyebrow and on my chin. I ran home screaming, but by the time I walked in the door, I was swelling up. I had never been stung before, but Mom said I was quite allergic to mosquito bites. She watched me, and I continued to swell up. The next morning I could not open my mouth, and couldn't see out of one eye.

It was sports day at school, and I was looking forward to it. I was told to stay home. Mom took me to the school to show the teachers how bad the swelling was, and I was so embarrassed, as it was hard to recognize me. Mom kept telling the teachers that this is serious. No kidding! Our doctor said if I were ever stung around the neck, it could be fatal. As if I needed something else to worry about?

In those days, Mom still performed most of the enemas on me. These were the years of training me to do it myself. My head was heavy with fluid from the swelling, and I had to be fed by a straw that we barely could get through my swollen lips.

Then the red hot heat and itching set in. Mom kept telling me to stop scratching, and I had pink calamine lotion all over my face. By the end of the week, my face was still swollen, and had numerous scratch marks all over.. After about two weeks finally the swelling went down, and my skin was hanging down my face like melted wax. Blood shot eyes were looking through the mess. I am really not a fan of getting stung around my face.

Exactly a year later, yes, one year later to the day, I was playing outside with my brothers when I was stung around my right wrist. My arm was so swollen, it seemed to be as big as a baseball bat. I could barely even lift it. I was only four feet tall and my weight was about 60 lbs. Oh, yes, it was the day before sports day again. Come on! Mom took me to the school again. At least, I could see and watch for a while. That arm itched for three or four weeks. My arm was bright red and hot to the touch with bee poison. Amazing a little bee can do this.

First Attempts

Around the age of eight, Mom started to teach me to do 'my thing', take my own enema. My grandmother suggested I try to lie on my left side, as she thought my bowel was on that side. Presently it is much easier to maneuver in this position. My first tries were not successful, and still to this day, the first enema I take is maybe only fifty per cent of the time partially successful.

As a youngster, I remember taking an enema, trying to find the opening, figuring out how to release the water from the bucket, only to realize the water was much too hot. I must have reacted as if I burned myself. I couldn't cool it down as the hot water was already inside. I must have scalded the inside of my bowel. Ouch, don't you just love one's mistakes?

I remember being very nervous after this. I then tried the squat, and it ended up making a hell of a mess, and falling or more like slipping off the toilet. I stopped doing the squat. Eventually, through trial and error, I learned how to test the water temperature, and get up off the floor while not losing so much of the water, and *stuff* from inside.

As I do not have a sphincter muscle for control, I had to quickly learn to squeeze my buttocks, in order to hold as much in as possible. Once again still a challenge, but I do have a nice strong pair of gluteus maximus due to 63 years of squeezing.

Yes, this is the messy part, shit happens, and too often, I wish it happened more often. I can only hope this would happen naturally. It is especially fun when the water bucket or a can would fall down on me. This would of course hurt. In the early days I used a hard porcelain bucket to draw water from that was hung from a nail above my head. On several occasions either the nail came loose from the wall, or the bucket handle slipped off the nail. In either case, I got very wet and usually some of the water that was already in me came out due to the surprise.

My parents finally took some holiday time alone, away from kids. Of course, being young, I really didn't know how important it was to try and have a successful enema daily. I would skip it. My stools backed up, and once I leaked on the floor. I had physical feelings like I was ready to have a bowel movement, but I also thought it was just gas, so I would push. My upper bowel is still able to have contractions thus causing cramps and a feeling like I can pass gas. This is when I was prone to leakage. I remember trying to clean things up with my Raggedy Ann doll's feet so my babysitter would not suspect I was skipping my daily duty. These days eventually caught up to me.

1956-Hippity Hop

As a young little "Hippity Hop" I would play, run, learn how to ride a bike, ski, sketch, write poems, sing and basically live a super life. We had moved to Canada, and I was learning about what it meant to be an Irish "O'Leary". I was very tiny, and people would often remind me of this.

I didn't really notice any difference from my friends at private school. Along with my classmates I got to celebrate my first communion, confirmation and found the nuns fascinating. In grade one during mass Sister Mary Lucinda used castanet's to remind us what to do and when. My memory of her brings back such love. At the end of our school day Sister would hug each child while telling us something positive. I truly felt she was an angel.

Although I loved being with my older and younger brother, I really wanted a sister. I was vaguely aware that I'd had a twin sister, but I was only just learning what that meant. When my mother was pregnant again, I was in grade four, and I constantly prayed that she would have a little girl. My mother was radiant when she was pregnant. She was a beautiful and fashionable woman, and wore high heels when she was expecting my little sister. She still wears high heels at ninety years of age!

My father wrestled with us -we called that vice- and he played hide and seek, sang and danced with us. When he arrived home from his business trips, we all would squeal with delight. These were truly happy times. My father nicknamed me "Hippity Hop" because I rarely would walk through the kitchen, as I constantly looked at the linoleum square patterns as a kind of hop scotch game. I skipped everywhere, my pony tail flopping up and down. I remember being in constant playful movement.

1960 - Listen to That Voice

I believe I acquired some 'street smarts' from my previous hospital experience's which helped me in this very scary situation while in elementary school. I had to take the bus home without my escort, the high school girl my parents hired to accompany me home, to protect me. I guess she had something to do, and she felt I could manage the three busses on my own from my school to our family home. I was in grade three or four. I knew the bus I needed was the number 20 Granville bus. I stood at the bus stop in my uniform waiting.

A transit bus came along that had an 'out of service' sign displayed, but to my surprise it stopped right in front of me, and the door opened. The driver offered to take me to any place I needed to go. Even though I felt 'This does not feel right', I got on the bus.

I ask myself today, 'Why did I not listen to that voice?'

The bus was empty, just the driver. I went to the back of the bus and sat down. He started an odd conversation with me. I ignored him as best I could. He asked me to move to the front of the bus, so he wouldn't have to yell. I did not move at first. He was persistent. I gave in again and moved behind him with the curtain between us.

Then he asked me to move across the aisle, so he could see me. The conversation turned to his daughter and that she also wears a uniform to school, and she wore bloomers. He asked if I wore bloomers. I didn't respond through all of his questions.

We were travelling north down Granville Street and one stop light from entering the Granville St. Bridge. He asked me if I would show him what I wore under my tunic. He was trying to convince me that after all he was a dad and helped his daughter dress in the morning. It would be okay.

I remember freaking out. Even though I was on a main street in a very large bus, I felt trapped. He had to stop at the next stop light as it turned red. I was sitting by the door, and I saw a lady right outside the door ready to cross the street in front of the bus. I started to scream, "This is not my bus, let me off! He is not a bus driver."

The lady heard this, and luckily for me started to pound on the door which startled him. She yelled at him to let me out. I was screaming, "Let me off the bus." Thank God, he did. Mostly, thank God for that lady.

The lady seemed to sense what I was going through. She insisted on getting me on the right bus. I did not want to leave her side. I clung to her. She then proceeded to take me all the way to Park Royal, and handed me over to Mom.

At that point, Mom reported this to the school and police. Later we discovered the man had stolen the bus and pretended to be legitimate. I believe they must have caught him. Lord only knows what he might have done to me. Thank you to that very kind lady.

I had an acute awareness of the opposite sex, and luckily for me these bad experiences made me very leery of the 'creeps' out there that will tell girls what they want to hear just to get a 'feel', or more. I learned to demand respect!

Years later, even while dating, I was sensitive to any wrong clues. However, I have been blessed with men in my family who have always been good, kind, respectful, gentle and loving.

1962 Elementary School - Poisonings

I had been moved to the Catholic girl's school in Vancouver for which I took 3 busses to and from home and school every day. This was the beginning of multiple hospital visits and puberty had come to my life. Lucky me!

I had just returned to school following a vaginal surgery. Lucky for me the staff were Nuns or lay women. They were all very supportive, but I still had to deal with my bowel issues.

I remember sitting at my desk wearing the school uniform navy blue tunic, tie, black tights and black oxford shoes. I felt sick and called my Mom. I always tried to sound like I could manage, and tried to demonstrate I was strong, as in, 'Don't cry.' Mom said she was busy, asked if I could manage to take the bus home, three busses, a long trip, yes three busses, but I agreed. I was in grade 6, what did I know? I should have gone to the hospital. I was training my brain to think I could manage any situation. 'I will not be a burden', I repeat, 'I will not be a burden!'

I make it through the first bus ride, and am now sitting next to the window at the back of the second bus. The buses only came by every half hour, so I had to get on that one. Not more than a mile down an extremely busy Georgia Street, the bus lurching forward, stop and go, stop and go, I leaned out of the window, and to the horror of the poor driver beside of the bus, and I projectile vomited and hit his car, as well as a lady standing innocently on the side of the curb.

My bus driver didn't know what was happening, so, of course, he just proceeded towards Stanley Park. I pulled my head back into the bus, and it seemed like everyone on the bus was looking back at me, probably in relief I didn't vomit inside the bus. No one wanted to come near me as they thought I had the flu.

What I was actually going through was one of my regular system poisonings! I never spoke with the lady or man in the car with his windshield covered in vomit. It was so very embarrassing! Oh my gosh, if either of you are reading this, I am so very sorry. Looking back, it is kind of sick funny!

Surgery I Remember

1962 Puberty

At eleven years old, I noticed when I slept on my stomach, still my preferred position today, I felt like I had rocks under my chest. Of course Mom had prepared me for puberty in some ways, but not for the actually feeling of growing breasts. When I was riding my bike with friends and ran into the boys, one of those fine 'gentlemen' made some comment about my boobs. "Hmmm", Mom said, "There'd be days like this."

Mom had told me about menstrual cycles and all of what a period entails. I remember having cramps that lasted about one week. I was eleven and I didn't think to mention it to Mom. Around a month later, I was in a lot of pain, and for the previous week had felt ill. Hmmm, this was another new thing for me to figure out at such a young age. The pain in my stomach got considerably worse, but the cramps subsided a little from time to time during that week.

Having been born with no exits. The surgeries had corrected the urethra and the anus, but there was not enough space for the menstrual cycle blood to flow out. I apparently had been bleeding the month before, and the blood was still in me. Now, for the second month in a row my so to speak self-cleaning oven, really needed to get flushed and cleaned out.

The following month while in Mass on Sunday, I was doubled over with pain, and finally made my parents really listen to me. My stomach was distended and extremely sore, even to the touch. My parents called our family doctor to the house.

I was shocked at how I was being examined. My operations as I knew it would never be the same from that day forward. I had hit puberty! He explained to me it was time to see a gynecologist, and yes, with the gynecologist came more surgery to reconstruct my system, yet once again!

My poor Mom and Dad, they must have been beside themselves, thinking "Not again?" I really put them through so much, and I am truly sorry. They are the best, as was Dr. Fred Bryans, the gentle soul who took me through that series of surgeries.

1962 The Examination Rooms

Is it fun to have a vaginal examination? Hell, no! Is there a single woman on this earth that would enjoy these intrusive examinations? I don't think so!

Now men - listen to this! You have to understand something. Since women were little, most of us we were taught that if you sat with your legs apart especially in a skirt, then we were not lady-like. We were taught to sit with our knees together and to the side or cross our legs at the knee. However, were men ever taught to sit that way? Women were controlled and directed back in the day, and this was my proper upbringing.

There I am, eleven, told to go to the doctors when my period was coming, and I remember an old man, an old hospital, fat nurse and lying there looking at the holes in the soft ceiling tiles. When lying on the examining table, I got so I would count the tiles or the little holes in the ceiling tiles, something to do! This old man was to become my amazing lifesaving doctor, Head of the Department at Vancouver General, Dr. Bryant! I used to dread the request, "Can you scoot a little closer, can you let your legs out, and can you relax?"

I was so very young, and didn't really fully understand the questions. It was so very difficult for me at this age to go to the maternity ward and gynecology department. I felt people looked at me like I was some kind of freak, 'twelve and pregnant?' With my tummy swollen from the back ups, I probably did look pregnant!

At the time, I really did not know who this new doctor was, except that he was the doctor I had to see to help relieve the pain. On this occasion Mom didn't come in with me. In hindsight, I was so young that would have been nice. I specifically remember my doctor came in with this metal thing that looked like a *duck beak*, or a pair of pliers. Wow, "What is he going to do with that? Oh doctor, no, you're not!" Oh, yes, he did!

So what goes on in a little girls head during this absolute horror! I really put on a brave face, no maybe a look of shock. First you ask me to spread my legs – Really? But that means I'm bad, not a lady. Hey, you can't be a lady when you have a doctor putting foreign objects, swabs, fingers inside of your anus which is supposed to be the vagina.

That's right, not my vagina, except a little urethra to probe around in. Have they ever had that done to them before? When a doctor says to a young girl "This may be a little cold," that too is a definite understatement. It's not a 'little, it's a lot 'cold'. Then they take little samples (they actually cut little pieces of your insides) to check. Hell, I had no idea.

In the next few years, I had surgeries and kind of knew what to expect going in. There were some surprises, big needles with die for x-rays, six or seven young interns looking over my doctor's shoulders, and peering down and into me. Hey, for a little girl, I felt horrible. I did not want it, like it, nor was I able to get out of it and admit I was not a willing participant.

Maybe a year later, and once again I had difficulties. Off I go to the hospital with my Dad. He really did not know what to do with me in the hospital parking lot. I was screaming, "I don't want to go in there." He just kept on saying you are sick and need to go in.

It was Christmas, in fact Boxing Day. It just did not seem fair that I had to share my privates with all of those inquisitive minds. It's a university hospital, so of course I was like a unique never before viewed medical training video. I'm certain my poor dad would rather have been in his office or better yet on the golf course. But he persevered and convinced me of the necessity. And of course, I needed it. Sorry, Daddy. Really, I was such a scared young brat.

We took the elevator upstairs to a lovely hospital room. You know the lovely everything is a pale green room with granite cold, loud floors. Then the doors start revolving. People with needles to take blood, people to check blood pressure, people to let you know the time you will be going into surgery, very early the next morning.

Prior to my surgery, it was necessary to have my private parts, my upper legs and torso shaved. I did not have much pubic hair yet, still just starting into puberty. I was in absolute horror once again to have such an experience at such a young age, and with no forewarning. After a sleepless night, no food, fluids only that are supposed to empty your bowels, once again surrounded by care givers. They dress me in a special gown with those very special green stockings that don't really fit, and top it off with a hair cap, and the *full monte'* exposure at the back of the gown…a look I have always strived for!

The IV is inserted, a shot to relax me is administered, and then the medical staff lifts me from my bed to the gurney. They are very sweet and have funny jokes to put me at ease. I am scared to death, and I try to joke back with them that make me feel more at ease. At Vancouver General, the halls go on for miles. The basement has miles of underground halls. These halls have colored lines painted on the floors leading to different departments. Mostly they look like they go to surgical theatres, OR, whatever they're called.

We arrive at our destination, and the electric doors that open quietly. There in front of me is my doctor – all dressed up. He speaks kindly to me. The surgical staff are moving around efficiently, occasionally saying soothing things to me. The lights over the surgery bed are very big, bright and scary. I'm placed on the operating table, my arms are strapped down - as if I am going anywhere - and another shot is administered. See you on the other side, I'm out.

Surgical Reports 1962 to 1963

December 27, 1962
Vancouver General Hospital
Dr. F.E. Bryans

Abdonimal Mass, Operation Performed E.U.A.

At the time of the cystomscopic examination carried out by Dr. Ankenman, an opportunity was taken to examine this patient under anesthesia. The external genitals appeared, on initial inspection, to be unremarkable apart from a somewhat anterior location of the single opening between the labia. This small caliber opening lay at the anterior limit of the external genitals. The details of the exploration of this aperture are described by Dr. Ankenman. The remainder of the examination under anesthesia relates to rectal examination and rectoabdominal examination.

On bimanual examination it was possible to indentify a smooth, firm, tense, cystic structure, approximately the size of a three month pregnancy, which arose in the pelvis and was easily palpable inferior to the umbilicus. This structure was freely mobile and no adnexal masses could be identified. There was no definite cervix indentified at the lower pole of the tumour described, and it was noted that there was a distance of approximately 5 to 6 cms between the lower pole of the mass described and the vulvar opening.

It was the clinical impression at the time of the examination that this mass represented the uterus distended with retained menstrual blood. The obstruction to drainage was believed to be the absence of a vagina.

She withstood the operative procedure well and was returned to her room in good post-operative condition. End of Report

—

January 14, 1963

Reprint — From F.E. Bryans M.D. VGH to Dr. J. Mashal Lions Gate Hospital Re: Miss Patty O'Leary

This is just a note to bring you up-to-date concerning Patty. Since the cystoscopy and examination under anesthesia carried out on December 27th, 1962, we have had an opportunity to discuss the interesting gynecological problem presented, and I have received a reply from Dr. Willis J. Potts of Chicago, the surgeon who operated upon her at the age of 3. In reviewing the literature, it is apparent that Patty's case is almost unique in that the few reported cases of hematometra without a vagina did not co-exist with a urinary tract abnormality such as is noted in the urethra and bladder neck here, nor was there a co-existing anal problem. Although several suggestions were offered at our rounds concerning means of draining the uterus with a view to maintaining its potential function, it is obvious that all of these constitute a considerable risk to the urinary control which she now has working so satisfactorily. I have had two full discussions with Mrs. O'Leary, and she feels strongly that she does not want to gamble Patty's urinary control for a hypothetical chance of maintaining fertility. I must say that I am in sympathy with this point of view, despite the anatomical challenge that is presented in the creation of a vagina that might subsequently be functionally rewarded by a pregnancy.

The present plan is to admit Patty to the Health Centre on Tuesday, February 5th, for a laparotomy on February 6th. The operative procedure will likely be an abdominal hysterectomy. However, a final opinion as to the best surgical procedure must be deferred until the operative findings are better known. The delay in her admission is in part occasioned by the fact that her father is to be on an eastern trip until the end of February and would like to be here when his daughter is operated upon. I felt that this delay was permissible as Patty has been comfortable without significant recurrence of the pain she had in December. Although I believe this to be a hematometra one cannot exclude the possibility of an unrelated pelvic tumour, so I will be happy to get on with the operation on the date mentioned above. I will confirm with you the time of the operation after admission. End of Report

—

February 6, 1963

Operation Reprint VGH Dr. F.E. Bryans, Dr. P.G. Ashmore, Congenital Absence of Vagina, Laparotomy, Drainage of Haematocolopos by Creation of an opening between the Vagina and the Urogential Sinus.

The patient was prepared and draped in the supine position. The abdomen was opened through a right paramedan incision with the removal of a previous cutaneous scar. On entering the peritoneal cavity and the freeing of fine omental adhesions to the posterior surface of the abdominal wall to the pelvic viscera, it was possible to recognize the double uterus with a complete septum. The tubes and ovaries on either side were of normal character and size. There was a corpus luteum visible in the left ovary. The pelvic mass which had been previously palpated on bimanual and rectal abdominal examination proved to be a grossly distended vagina. There was no evidence of hematometra or distention of the tubes, but the vagina was markedly distended.

An incision was made at the posterior surface of the upper vagina and a large amount of dark red jelly-like retained menstrual secretion was removed. The character of the menstrual retained blood indicated considerable long standing collection and the partial break-down of the blood had evidence by its reddish brown character and its jelly-like consistency. With a finger through the opening created on the posterior surface of the distended vagina, it was possible to explore a large distended vagina and to identify a blind sac at the lower end. It was then decided an attempt would be made to drain the obviously relatively complete vagina through the deficient lower end into the urogenital sinus. With a finger in the vagina, it was possible also to identify the presence of a septum and although two cervices were not definitely confirmed, it is believed that this girl has double uterus, double cervix and a longitudinal vaginal septum which extends 1-2 inches down into the vagina.

With a finger in the lower end of the urogenital sinus, it was possible to recognize that the space separating the urogenital sinus and the lower end of the vagina was very thin. It was thus recognized that the congenital abnormality here was not the absence of the vagina.

Note: Surgical pathology report identified the small black lesion from anterior abdominal wall near line of laparotomy incision was a benign compound nevus of skin of abdomen.

End of Report

—

February 18, 1963

Letter Reprint VGH Dr. F.E. Bryans to Dr. W.J. Potts, The Children's Memorial Hospital Chicago, Re: Miss Patty O'Leary

Thank you very much for your informative letter of January 7th concerning the management of Patty while in Children's Memorial Hospital. You will be pleased to learn that she has had virtually no trouble with the renal tract in the intervening years. She is a very bright and normal little girl, who is rapidly becoming a young lady. Herein lays the source of the difficulties which have recently brought her under attention. She is showing the secondary sex characteristics now at the age of 12, and in recent months has developed approximately cyclical crampy abdominal pain. On abdominal and recto-vaginal examination it was possible to recognize a palpable mobile semi-cystic tumour in the pelvis which was approximately the size of an 8 to 10 week pregnancy. As there is only one perineal opening which initially was interpreted as benign the urethra, a diagnosis of hematometra or hematocolpos was made. At cystoscopic examination, the bladder was found to be perfectly normal, and although somewhat elongated the balder neck was felt to be within normal limits. No perineal aspect of the vagina could be visualized, and the lower end of the pelvic mass initially seemed to be well removed from the perineal floor. A laparotomy was performed about 10 days ago, at which time it was recognized that she had a double uterus but had normal tubes and ovaries. The mass described was a grossly distended vagina, confirming the diagnosis of hematocolpos. An incision was made through the posterior wall of the vagina, and the contents were drained abdominally. It was then possible to explore the distended vaginal cavity, and on palpation of recognize that the lower limit of the blind sac came to with ½ cm. of tissue separation the lower end of the perineal tube which must be a urogenital sinus. It was possible to break through this separating tissue and to provide drainage for the vagina. In the future, it should not be difficult to enlarge this vaginal opening and to create a functioning vagina. It was also noted at the time of the opening of the vagina that she had a transverse septum and two cervices so that she has normal development but lack of fusion of the two Mullerian duct components of her genital canal. From my reading I gather that the combination of congenital absence of the lower end of the vagina in association with an imperforate anus is an extremely rare anomaly. Her rectal problem presents very little difficulty beyond the need for daily enemas. I am hoping that her genital tract will cause here a little future concern.

Mr. and Mrs. O'Leary speak highly of your interest in Patty,
and wish to be remembered kindly to you.

End of Report

After my reconstructive surgery so I could have a period, I had a lousy time adjusting to the amount of flow. I mean the sanitary pads hardly did any good. I was changing all day for the first two days. Also the pads would smell of dead fish. Mess and smells are one of the costs of motherhood I was told. Now I had two areas of body odors to contend with. I was not able to wear tampons yet, so the outside clothes were also soiled. At twelve years of age, I don't think I did a very good job. Thank goodness for toilet paper. A great thing to carry around and use when needed.

A Light Came On - Molested

While at the hospital — about a month this time- I had a very weird experience, and to this day, I wish I was older at the time of the incident. I was a victim of another weird, but good lesson in life. I'm proud of how I handled myself.

Mom, once again a living saint, had warned me at a very young age about strangers, and if you feel something isn't right, you are probably correct, and should listen to my instincts and act. OK, so there I was, eleven years old lying in my bed. Due to my enemas, they gave me a private room, rather than a ward bed.

The hospital was quiet except for the typical noises of the night, quiet voices at the nurses' station, trolleys pushed down the hall that carried meds, blood test vials, and nurses carrying supplies for the early morning operations to come. Sometimes they would gently bump against the fender boards along the halls issuing a mild clink and clang of the vials pushing against one another. I was partially drugged due to my surgery scheduled for the next morning.

The nurses would do their rounds, but mostly with flash lights: give meds, check catheters and I.V. and N.G. tubes late at night. This usually took place about 12:30 after a shift change, so I didn't react right away to the small light turned on over my headboard. I woke up to a man standing over my bed.

It was still pretty dark in the room. I remember he was wearing, a striped shirt, red suspenders and thick glasses, but I couldn't see his eyes. He spoke very quietly. He said he had come in to make an examination. I was used to my doctor, the head of gynecology. I was confused, as this was a stranger. I thought 'Where is my doctor? And why is he waking me up so late at night?'

He lifted up my gown to check my stomach, touched my breasts, and then he wanted to check even lower. He tried to put his hand up my vagina, and I once again felt a weird feeling, nauseating feeling — this was not right. I asked, "Where is my Doctor? Where is the nurse?"

I had been showing my privates to doctors and interns, but usually my main specialist always had a female assistant to observe. My doctor occasionally would bring that entourage of young men interns to talk with me and do some checks. Not just a question answer period, sometimes he would lift up my gown to check a few things out in front of them. After all they were in a university hospital, and they were there to learn. I really hated that, really!

His fingers were probing my crotch now, and I thought I would be sick to my stomach. Once again I forcefully asked, "Where is the nurse?" The pervert intern just stopped and walked out.

I listened towards the nurses' station, and heard no conversation, then covered myself and went back to sleep. When the nurse came in with her flashlight for a nightly check, she asked me why my light was on. Of course, I told her the doctor put it on. She had a confused look on her face, and then quietly said, "It's ok, just go back to sleep."

Scary stuff, as there was no locked doors in the hospitals in those days or locked rooms either. Of course, Medical staff has to quickly get to the patients when they are needed. OK, I am taking a very long deep breath, remembering this one.

I felt nauseous and scared. But I never talked to my parents about it because I truly thought he was a doctor. Then later while explaining this to my sister, I figured it out. How did he know where I was, how did he know a young girl would not question him like an adult? Then it hit me. I would imagine he was one of those interns. He could just slip in by the nurses; also he knew exactly where I was and that I was partly drugged from my surgery preparation, likely he was not an intern at all. The man was in a disguise, and not a very good one at that. If he was an intern, I would have seen him during the rounds. He was a jack ass from the street, not someone I felt I could trust.

I was once again just trying to be brave and not be a difficult patient, but a cooperative one. Why did I feel sick? But I felt sick a lot, so I was confused. Make no mistake, I now know as clear as day, years later, I was sexually molested!

As a patient, I was so used to people checking on me. In fact many times even to this day, I have doctors and nurses asking the same questions that may have been asked only an hour before or the last operation. Whenever the door of my hospital room would open, it was either doctor wanting to give me good or bad news, technicians wanting to take more blood —this happened sometimes during the middle of the night—shots for pain, or just the cleaning staff.

The good times were when family or friends would come in; I always looked forward to their company. Also I would be elated when I was finally able to eat, the food: fabulous hospital food.

As I was growing up, I really did not discuss my health with my friends. These experiences are extremely humiliating; they are the times I had to think on my feet or in some cases swim. You have to have a sense of humour!

1963 13 years Old

I had problems with my periods each month with a day or two of heavy hemorrhaging. In Grade Eight, public school, science class, and wearing a pleated green skirt, I start to bleed, bleed and bleed.

I was just sitting on this tall dark green lab stool. There is a pool of blood on the stool, and luckily I'm at the back of the class. I asked a friend—something I have had to learn to do—to walk behind me to the office. Once again I leave school and go home.

Mom wanted me to go back to school, but I knew everyone would see I was not wearing the same clothes. I was missing a day of school for every period, and the counselors had to inform the teachers of my health situation. The teachers were supportive and ready to let me leave their class to change in the bathroom. It was messy and very stressful.

I started to ask myself if this is normal. I didn't know others who needed to leave the school just because it was their period. I started to ask my friends and listen closely to what they had to go through when they had their monthly "visitor". I was learning I was not necessarily in control of another part of my body. I was trying to learn self acceptance, and did not like more loss of bodily control.

Self Acceptance and Success!

In 1963 I started ski racing in Grade Eight on the local mountain ski team. This meant travel to different areas for competitions and staying in dorm-like situations and sharing bathrooms and showers, etc. I really was not too keen on telling my male coaches and team mates what my evenings are like, and how much sleep I would miss. I was afraid this would affect the coach's decisions about my participation. I did not even tell my Mom and Dad.

Through high school I did some school races, and basically told mountain team mates I did not feel well. I was very embarrassed and could not go to the coach, and could not look them in the eye. I just slipped away; I was one of those athletes, a quitter. When I became a coach myself, I remember those athletes that I had to chase down, the girls that were a disappointment, and girls that wasted their talent, and yes, the girls that wasted my precious time. Sad, I did not want to be remembered as one myself.

I was struggling to compute my roll in this world. I was realizing I would be hop scotching my way through life in search of who I was and who I would be. I did not want to fall off that path; I did not handle losing well. The worst part is I would appear to be the athlete that wastes the coach's time. It was a worry for me how people would look at, or think of me. I was picky who I would explain or talk to about my kidneys, period issues or bowel dysfunctions.

Younger Perversion

I was in the children's ward. I was once again lying in my bed, and the door slowly opened. It was dark. This young boy around 14 or 15 came in my room. He started a conversation with me. You know the usual questions. "What grade are you in? What are your interests?"

He and I had passed in the hall a few times. I had not said anything to him, but he knew where I was. He surely observed I had tubes everywhere, and I was vulnerable. I thought the hospital would be safe. I never really worried about my security. I had enough on my mind.

He continued to ask "Where were my tubes going in and how they worked?" Yes, he would ask simple enough questions, but he started to ask questions that made my antennae go up. He acted curious and wanted to know if I would show him where these tubes were connected on my body.

The next thing I knew he was climbing in bed with me. Luckily, even though I had a catheter, I.V. and feeding tubes, I had powerful legs, and I had just one message for him – kick, kick, and kick again! I don't care if he was sick —- I was not going to let him near me. He landed on the floor. He cursed and then left.

I reported this to the nurses. I asked the nurses if they could lock the doors. They said, "No, but they would keep an eye out for any further intrusions."

The nurses explained how this boy had some problems, really? People did feel sorry for his family, but what disgusts me is the fact people seemed to feel sorry for the guy and would not worry about me at that point. North Americans are too soft. We need to send a message: be aware, protect and punish!

I believe the only times I slept well was during the day were after my family visited, or when I was drugged for pain. The children's ward was not a great place to be. Some of my worst memories are from those operations. I was always worried about some of the other children I met. There was crying mostly at night that drifted down the dark hallways exposing the prevalent fear of the unknown.

1964 *Growing Adjustments*

Grade nine, fourteen years old, still struggling with my periods, I would have heavy days; however, I wanted to ignore my body's weaknesses and to try out for the school track team. I went to track practice, and it was the start of my period. I had some really good results in the time trials, and the coach asked me to run against the boys to see if I could get my times down even further.

After practice I arrived home to bad cramps, finished my homework, took my enema, and went to bed. In the middle of the night, I woke up feeling like I had bowel problems. Mom looked in on me as it was unusual for me to go to bed so early. She turned on the light to a horrible surprise: the top of my covers were covered in blood. She pulled back the blanket to see that I was lying in a very large pool of blood, and I was still bleeding.

For a few days Mom changed my sheets continuously day and night, then off to the hospital I went. I was told I did not need surgery, but that I should not run or exercise. So something that was probably good for me was now *verboten*, forbidden. Of course I was devastated. Something I was very good at was now supposed to end. Luckily I didn't really listen to them. So what's a little hemorrhage?

I went back to our male track coach to tell him, and he really did not appreciate my excuses. He thought I was just a quitter and couldn't handle running with the guys. Then for more embarrassment, the boys on the team kept asking me what was wrong, why was I not training with them anymore. Evidently, they were told by the coach I was the fastest female in the school. 'Whatever!'

All through high school my periods were quite regular, but extremely uncomfortable and heavy. For me wearing white pants was not an option at that time.

Sixteen and Scared

In my sixteenth year, I tried to ignore a series of infections, headaches, pain and bloating. Mom was in the hospital with a collapsed lung, and my father was away for business. I had exams to study for and was having a discharge that looked like puss. Sixteen, scared and hoping this would all just go away. I did not want my parents to worry. Fortunately for me Dad was only gone for a few days as he was needed at home to care for Mom.

That morning Mrs. Mugget, a close family friend, was so very worried about me that she drove really fast on route to the doctor's office. I was vomiting from the infection and was very dizzy. Then we heard the siren, and the police pulled us over. In panic, she spoke about how much I was hemorrhaging.

I was too sick to really care about what the policeman would think. The policeman escorted us, and we arrived at the doctor's office in record time. Once the doctor examined me, I was rushed across the city to Vancouver General. More doctors and tests meant more delays. I really thought I was going to --- and wanted to die.

Mrs. Mugget left once I was in my hospital bed. I was alone and really didn't know what was happening to me. I was told by my specialist's intern I was immediately going in for major surgery. I have to add, I found her comments to be so very matter of fact! No bedside manner there. I didn't know the intern, what I really wanted was a hug and was scared to death. As per the course, they started to prep me, shaving and swabbing on the red disinfectant all over my tummy.

I really needed my Mom! But she was going through her own hell, and was probably thinking the same. I did get to speak with her by phone from the nurses' station. I tried to be brave, but broke down when I heard her voice. Anyway, she really did not want me to cry and told me to be brave. I remember her saying once again, "*Patty doesn't cry!*" I must say that was easier said than done. I really wanted to appear brave for everyone else, but mostly this was a good training for 'Chin up Patricia, you have to do this.' As I have said, I was scared so much that I really did not cry.

I was learning an important lesson in life, having to handle things on my own. I was gaining strength and recognizing it. This was a form of success. I was learning to live in every small success, rather than accepting any failures.

I remember walking back to the room, not used to not having Mom with me. We had to rely on friends and our faith. By the way, that works really well! I was always told to not cry. I guess that was to train me to be brave.

I do believe now at my ripe old age of 63 that when in the state of tears, we let our guard down and we communicate deep thoughts and feelings. Just the other day, my mother stated tears are not a good thing. I disagreed with her. I believe in some tears for release, then focus on positive images of next week or month. For her, she must have had to teach herself to not cry. I have not seen her cry much, and she is now 90. She is amazing.

November 11, 1967

VGH Dr. F. E. Bryans - Congenital Vaginal Deformity/ Examination under anesthesia and dilatation of vaginal opening.

The patient was prepared and draped in the lithotomy position. This 17 year old girl who has a congenital abnormality of the lower vagina and rectum underwent a rectal repair as an infant and in 1963 had a laparotomy with the drainage of a large hematocolpos and establishment of a drainage point from the lower end of her vagina through the perineum. She has had regular menstrual periods in the intervening four years and had a normal menstrual period approximately two weeks ago. At the conclusion of this period she developed lower abdominal pain and fever.

On abdominal examination there was a palpable suprapubic mass approximately the size of a 4-6 week pregnancy and on rectal examination a tense swelling that was interpreted as being a distended vagina was noted. A purulent vaginal discharge could be identified on inspection of the shallow vagina as coming from an almost pinpoint opening at the vault of the vagina.

Using Hegar dilators this opening was dilated until a size 10 Hegar could be inserted. With each progressive increase in dilatation there was the escape of a large amount of purulent material and the gradual reduction in the size of the palpable pelvic mass. A Foley catheter was placed in the cavity which was believed to be a distended vagina and the cavity was irrigated.

The explanation for her findings is that she has had gradual closure of the vaginal opening and with this progressive increase in retention of blood which has become infected. With the dilatation and the free drainage it is hoped a recurrence of this phenomenon will not occur.

She withstood the procedure well and was returned to her room in good post operative condition. End of Rep

Really?

A week later the medical staff came in to let me know they had to go in again to do some clean up. This time I believe they again went in vaginally. You get the picture. I was in for more fun and games. I recall my vaginal area burned for ages after that. I am just saying! In the hospital for about three weeks, and yes, more time away from school and my studies.

Happier Times

Even at this young age of 16, I wanted to feel in control and empowered. As a ski instructor and now with a driver's license, I felt I was on my way. I was growing up. From time to time my parents had me drive my younger siblings to school or the store. I know how much this probably helped our clan. I did the same with my children.

I would also drive myself to work, and as a ski instructor at Grouse Mountain, was not about to ask my parents to drive me at 6:30 a.m. Of course living up in the British Properties meant that at that time of year I would of course, wake up to a dark day and to brand new snow. I learned to maneuver the big car down a steep windy driveway and slip slide my way to the Upper Levels highway, and then make my way back up to Grouse.

One day while standing in front of my class, we were getting soaked with rain. The snow was sticky and in my opinion very dangerous for a beginner group. I decided to cancel the class and give them two makeup classes at another time. I also promised I would buy them all a hot chocolate. I was learning business marketing, right? I took the gondola down to the parking lot, noticing that the rain was not stopping, and knew the parking lot would be tricky to walk on. Luckily I had my old muckluc boots with good traction. As I looked out on the parking lot, all the cars were slowly moving sideways, one even backwards down the gradual parking lot hill. It was very eerie looking at the large metal machines sliding slowly without drivers.

I made my way to my car, slowly pushed it away from another car it had slid into on the driver's side. I calmly unlocked it and climbed in while it still slowly continued to slide down the grade.

My old stick shift 1958 Volvo was a cool car and heavy. I started her up, put it in reverse and slowly came to a stop right by the wall of ice I had been sliding towards. In my rear view mirror I noted, OMG here they come – cars, moving on down the hill towards me. My heart rate jumped up. I put my car in a faster mode and turned it away from the wall of ice and managed to dodge the cars and got out of there!

At that moment in time, I was in control; I thought on my feet and took on a challenge I probably would never encounter again. I was empowered! I shouted a few things: such as "You rock Patricia!" "Holy S--- that was close."

Of course I called the ski school to get crews out there to sand, and then I watched a few cars crash. It was just weird.

When I went through my health issues a few months later, I used this parking lot experience to steal strength, to jump on it, to feel in control.

1966 – California Cousins

I'm sixteen years old and in California at an aunt and uncle's home for a visit. I am sleeping in the pull-out bed in the family room where everyone in their family can see me in the morning. Once I must have coughed after my enema. It's a dangerous trend with me and I emptied all over under the covers. Their dog would not leave me alone that morning.

My uncle, bless his heart, blamed it on the dog and wondered what everyone had fed it thinking that poor, innocent animal had soiled their carpet somewhere. I just laid there in panic while he roamed the room looking for the smelly evidence. The dog wanted to mount the bed and search under my covers. OMG I was mortified!

My aunt came in, and I started to cry. I thought I could handle just about anything, but the dog was big and would not go away. My uncle put the dog out on their back porch. I called my aunt over and told her what really had happened. She was a nurse and knew what to do, asking my uncle to take the rest of the family out for breakfast.

A week later down at Balboa Bay, I was to stay with my other cousin Christine, on my Mother's side of the family. This included staying on our grandfather's sail boat. This also meant dealing with boats flying around us at all hours, her boyfriend visiting and of course, taking enemas in the "head".

This bathroom is literally the size of a chair, a very small chair. It is way too small. So I had to kick everyone out of the galley to take my "thing", then I would lie on the galley floor, and later climb into the very small bathroom. Needless to say, I skipped the glorious "thing" as much as possible, I chose to. It was a decision to save me embarrassment due to my smells and sounds.

What a great time we had. We sat on the top of the cabin bathing in the warm California sun, and every day we would go to the nearby beaches to body surf. I basically treaded water all day and crashed on the beach. I thoroughly enjoyed the chance to flirt with the boys and stay up very late at night. We were lucky our grandfather let us stay on our own.

My grandfather Bopo did check in on us a lot. He took us for lunch and left us pretty much to fend for ourselves until I lost the ore lock overboard, literally a second after he warned me about it. Also I knocked over a carton of milk in the back seat of his car. The temperature outside was around 98 degrees. It was at this point in time that we were sent back to my aunt and uncle's place. Hmm, is it something we did, could it have been the sour smell of milk? Perhaps! It was just as well I needed to take care of my health.

I must admit my cousin was terrific. She was already used to sharing the bathroom at her parent's house with the rest of the family, six of us, including, their cat.

1969 Yet More Surgery

Dr. Ankerman identified urethra infections, and upon examination, a knuckle in the bowel was discovered resulting in surgery during my high school senior year exams. The surgery was a major clean up. Dr. Ankerman opened up a few areas that were blocked by thickened blood. He went through vaginally, and I must say this type of surgery really is not fun. Stitches, stitches and more stitches. When you have stitches in or around the vagina, the healing is a slow itchy torture.

Surgery Preparations and Reflections

Preparations – they are a scary experience, but I know the healing can be more challenging than the actual surgery. Usually, I slept through most of my surgeries and procedure.

This is what usually happens from post op major surgery. I awake to the sound of a soft voice. "Patty, how are you doing?" I am in the recovery room. I drift in and out of consciousness. I'm back in my room; I'm lucky, I have family waiting. I am alive; I knew I'd be Ok! Thank you, for modern medicine, and prayer.

After the surgery, I'm drugged to the nines. I open my eyes to get a sip of water and ice cubes. My mouth feels dry, and my throat is sore from NG tubes or whatever. I don't need to worry about going to the bathroom. I have tubes that help with that.

Day 1: the nurses seem to think I can sit up. After major surgery, that is the last thing you want or feel like doing. This can cause nausea and dizziness, but it really is the best thing to do. Not to mention, if you just had your stomach cut open, there is pain, lots of pain. Getting back to the sitting up part, it does clear the cobwebs and gets the mind thinking, 'Ok, I can reach that water or, I can – and I will get stronger.'

Day 2: It's when you really feel the need for more Tylenol 3's or whatever they put in those shots that put me in La La land. The nurse called the pain killer one thing when I was young, but as I grew older, it became my 'Evening Cocktail!' in her words.

The pain from surgery varies with each operation that is abdominal, vaginal, or a severed Achilles tendon. When you get a shot for pain every four hours, what they should say is "You will be in a lot of pain for about three hours, until we walk in the door with your pain relief again."

Day 3: I really need more pain killers? Over the next few days, the pain diminished, and by the seventh day, sometimes you get over the hump to feel like you can start to mend. Then I would usually let the nurses know I did not want any heavy drugs anymore.

About three days into my recovery, the physiotherapist told me it was time to walk. It was a buildup of the first two days, when they had worked with me. Ouch everywhere!! Standing isn't easy with the influence of very strong drugs and a very sore body. "Are you serious I want to ask.' So I told them, "I have just had major surgery, cut right open? Shaking and to support my incision, I hold my stomach with one hand. I swing my legs over the side of the bed slide down onto my feet, take a step or two, then I fall right back on the bed. I was asked to do this over and over again, I was gaining strength. I was in training again.

No one told me that when you have surgery in the private area, that the fresh stitches, swelling, the pubic hair growing back in would itch like crazy! I was strapped up quite a bit with nasal gastrointestinal tubes, IV tubes, drainage and nutrition tubes so that I could not scratch the itch to my satisfaction.

About the third day with no showers, my hair was so very greasy that it smells and feels gross. It is a different smell, and it seems to be everywhere. My elbows have rug burns due to the constant shifting to sit up on the very coarse hospital sheets. I told myself; this is like you're a camper or a bit of a dirty-cool hippie roughing it feeling. I needed to have thoughts to trick myself, to give me time for healing. However, I am a girl that showers often. I admit that even after just a day or even five days; it gets to a point where you say to yourself, "I need a shower, and I need it badly" In this circumstance, it was not up to me. Note those sponge baths don't really do the trick.

Day 5: At about five days, I am walking up and down the halls, still holding my stomach, along with the IV stand, and my catheter trailing like a wagging tail. On the fifth day, someone would finally wheel me to a sink and wash my hair. I was looking forward to not having an itchy scalp. I have to add that my groin area was screaming, 'clean this area.' What an amazing thought, and my mood improved just thinking about the process. It was almost, I mean, almost orgasmic!

Ahhh, to be clean again! I had to wait for two weeks for the actual shower. The orderlies would give me very intrusive sponge baths that made me feel somewhat better. However, the smell of the hospital had penetrated my skin: I stunk. My bed sores from lying down for so much time were raw and blistered. Usually I had to wait until my stitches were taken out before I could have a shower or bath. I knew when the stitches were taken out that I was on the mend.

Day 14: The next glorious day the nurse came in, looked at my incision and said, very happily, "Do you feel like giving yourself a shower-or even better a bath?"

A bath, OMG, please! So there I was walking down to the amazing big bathroom with a gigantic old tub and a window that looked over to the North Shore to my parent's house. The nurses helped ease me into the tub. They left me there to just relax, get clean and feel human again. I was alive!

With all of my Ops - Hunger

This is the time you really start to miss home, food and friendly company. I loved having a television to distract me, but the commercials with food would drive me bonkers. I even got up and walked down the hall to the dumbwaiter room and looked at plates of food where people had left scraps. I knew if I ate I would feel sick. I was still on fluids and not permitted to eat solids. But, the good thing was, well, I am losing weight. However, this is not the way to do it. I lost too much weight and, of course, muscle.

I was extremely weak and just wanted to sleep due to, the whole tiring process.

When I was in the hospital at the age of 38 for a hysterectomy, I recall a nurse coming into the room to find me standing on my bed, tubes everywhere, "What are you doing?" she asked.

"I'm looking to see how much weight I've lost. I can't see the mirror unless I stand on the bed!" I replied. I was looking for a reward for all of the crap I was going through.

I was on nutrition tubes, no fluids; etc. for quite a while to let my insides rest and get the swelling down. So I was hungry while losing muscle and fat quickly. I had no way of knowing how much. I just knew I was dwindling away.

I did, of course miss my sports and just moving around without being tethered to tubes. It was always a thrill to start to move, even with a shuffle or in a wheelchair. I have been in the hospital so much I actually would have a routine if you will. Wheelchairs were the best step to aid the process, to get out of bed for a change of scenery. This was also the only way I could move around. My visitors too would get to walk and talk. Another observation was I felt I needed to entertain visitors, so that they would come back. Between pain killers and during pain, I would try to make people feel comfortable while they were sitting there. I felt like I was on display or something.

Of course, when a person is fairly inactive and not eating, they are very weak. I was tired and needed naps. At this point, food was always on my mind. Was I empowered by all of this? Yes, in a weird way I was. I trained myself constantly by positive thoughts. 'You will get out, and you will have fun again. You, "Baby A" can wait this out, heal and you will live.'

Breakout day: This could be any time when I finally am permitted to leave the hospital. Of course, there was the visit from the doctors, the review of what I may expect for my health, bla, bla, bla. Then I had to gather all of my belongings. Then I put on the clothes I wore in to the hospital, and always, these items fell almost to the floor. I have lost weight and usually forget to change my 'going-home-clothes' to something smaller. Then I board the wheelchair, smile at my loved ones and am pushed by the desk, say my goodbyes and give thank you waves to the nursing staff.

Then once in the car; I am a nervous wreck due to my body which has not been really moving for so very long. I nag whoever is driving and am very jumpy. Then, I go into my own home and room. Ahhhh, just from the car ride I am extremely exhausted.

Now that I have had so much of my internal system rearranged, and taken out due to cysts and cancer warnings that when the doctors 'go down' to check, I think it echoes! 'Hey, Patty, you don't have much left down here, here, here.' (echoes).

I actually have a conversation with the doctors, "Does everything look ok?"

"For, for, you, you, you, it looks, oh, oh, okay."

Tedious Forms

Now as an adult whenever I go to the hospital for tests or a check up, and am given that long tedious admissions form to fill out, I smile. There is always the question, "Have you had any previous operations? and for what?"

'Come on really? I want to shout. Every time this happens, I laugh, and always just smile. I give a quick review...female surgeries, and intestinal disorders etc, and really don't go into all of it, especially if they are looking at something I know will not have anything to do with my insides.

Freedom- On My Own!

I was no longer going to always be under my parent's roof. I luckily had been permitted to go away for weekends with friends, as well as stay with relatives in California, etc., learning how to adapt with my body's inabilities while away from home as well as think on my own.

So off I went on a high school student tour to Europe with money I saved from babysitting and teaching skiing. We were going to be staying in school dorms in England, Germany, and Italy. Bathroom situations were something I knew I would figure out at the time; at least, I was naïve enough to think so. Next are a few stories of that summer.

Pull The Chain

Our first stop was England where we stayed at a beautiful college campus. The bathrooms were acceptable and provided some privacy. Then I travelled to Holland where the open toilet stall was a hole in the floor, with a flush mechanism that was a chain hanging from the ceiling. When pulled, water came out of the wall around the floor's edge. One had to squat over a hole the size of a normal shower drain. For an enema taker, this was not at all suitable. The lack of all of these necessities really caused stress for me. The result was my system backed up and caused poisoning, again.

I did however take the time to enjoy the European experience, the people, practicing my French and of course new cultures and the arts. We hopped on and off busses all day and proceeded to look in every nook and cranny down the cobble stone roads and alleys. I was in heaven with the beauty and history of the castles and churches.

The Red Baron

In 1969, the Vietnam War was raging, and fortunately my older brother was assigned duty in Germany. My plan was to travel with him, a friend of his, and a high school girl friend to Italy in a Volkswagen bug, the Red Baron.

Friend, Mary Anne P., and older brother Danny in Italy

Our only plan was to drive to the Vatican in Rome, Italy. We didn't know where we would stay, and my enema needs were not at the forefront of my older brother's mind or for that matter in any of our minds. We were young and away from our parents and teachers. We were so very wide eyed, somewhat inexperienced, and did not have a care in the world.

The first evening we were lost in the countryside, with no place to stay. We decided to camp out in a hilly forest. No camping gear, not even sleeping bags. I chose a soft sandy tree needle strewn area. Ah, the night was sleepless. My soft sandy spot was an ant hill. I had 50 or more ant bites that were irritated by my one piece coullot and shoulder straps. Yes, I was glad I did not try to take an enema out in the wild. We were absolutely miserable.

The sleepless night without having done 'my thing', ant bites, nausea from traveling in the overstuffed Red Baron, and my system backing up was creating havoc. I needed to rid myself of all of that great pasta and toxins from the night before. I finally lost it as the nausea and dizziness stayed for more than a day. At this point, my brother looked for a place to stay; he was worried, and frankly so was I. Ahhh, to take an enema that worked, I would be fine. Finally!

I have such amazing memories of visiting several European countries back in 1969. I was introduced to drinking beer and down comforters. I thought we were going to die so many times snaking our way through dangerous windy narrow roads. I was also thrilled about travelling with my older brother. Growing up as Catholics, he and I were blessed for this opportunity to visit Vatican City.

As an art student, I was thrilled to stare in amazement at famous artist's sculptures and paintings. My favorite was the Pieta in St. Peter's. It gave me such satisfaction after saving every penny; for three years as a baby sitter and ski instructor to experience many sights, sounds and smells. I was easily distracted from my health issues from the many new and amazing people and sights we saw along the way.

Feeding Fish

In Europe, swimming on a topless beach near Nice, France. While in the water with friends, I laughed so hard that I had a bowel movement right there in the beautiful blue water.

I was in about 4 feet of water, and suddenly a school of fish came from nowhere. There were hundreds of them. In a way I was quite grateful; they were cleaning up the water, but I was the only one all these colorful fish were surrounding. I swam away, and they followed me. I told everyone it must have been my colorful bathing suit. I don't think they bought that one.

I decided to swim out further to clean myself as best as possible. I couldn't face walking out of the water up the beach and have that mess dripping down my legs. Although with the naked people around, I rather doubt anyone was looking at the girl with 'poop.' Thank heavens, no sharks were in that water. Looking back, I have to laugh, I mean picture it. Sense of Humour!

Travel is very hard on me. Of course, when I take enemas, I just use the tap water, and of course, that's not a great idea in foreign lands. Now when we travel, I take into consideration the location, whether the tap water will be safe to drink, and then if it is, it should be okay for enemas.

I learned from a very young age, even if I skipped my enemas, my body continued to try to get rid of the waste; I would have fluid come out. I felt like I had upper bowel push, but not in the lower bowel. Now, I prefer to take my enema at night, so afterwards I can rest and not have to go anywhere. I can just be near the bathroom, just like if a person who has diarrhea.

So I learned to take toilet paper and plug the necessary area. This of course causes diaper rash, cramps, and forces trips to the can. Many times I soiled my clothes. Many times I would soil bedding, and this was not fun when away from home. Numerous times I have had to leave school, friends and activities to return home to care for my 'liquid departures'. Now I buy paper towels as part of my kit when I travel. They come in handy for the enemas, so I don't have to use towels that are supplied. Also the towels are handy if I need them for the bed to protect sheets.

A Singing Career?

I always thought there was potential in a singing career. On my own I trained constantly during high school, and fitting with the times, 1960's, played the piano and guitar. I sang solo and in groups. Could've, would've, should have acquired an agent, but I didn't know where to go for guidance. At sixteen I was in L.A. and had an opportunity to sing in a night club/coffee house, but I did not like to sing where there was so much cigarette smoke. Perhaps this was an opportunity missed.

My vocal reputation linked me up to sing at weddings, group meetings and seminars, high schools, and on our college campus. In junior college, I had an instructor who praised me about how I should be an opera singer. Ah, I don't think so. Even so, I should have asked for more guidance or at least direction from this professor. At the time, I was getting a name in this small town and when people asked how much I charge I had no guidance. I just said, "Oh, $8.00 a song."

It was at this moment of my life where I should have been more proactive relative to my singing, and I just let the opportunity slip away as I got more involved in my training as a teacher. Positive note: I was able to yell at my students from far away and sing to them from time to time. I have really no regrets about not becoming a singing "star".

While away at school, my father kept tabs on my progress. He did not discourage my singing, but he wanted me to be able to take care of myself someday. I remember my father's motivational words, "Just make certain whatever you take at school, you can get a job. And don't take any underwater basket weaving classes." But, Dad, I did make $25.00 singing at a wedding or $16.00 for singing two songs at blab la bla. In other words, I needed to think about getting a real job one day, and so I did.

Off To College

An opportunity was presented to me to attend a junior college, but with no real academic arsenal. I had thoughts of being a nurse, and desperately wanted to move on to a four year university. Considering my high school struggles with my health and learning disabilities, I didn't have many choices, unless I created a new path for myself, a back door if you will.

There were not many options, so off I went to this beautiful small town, and a fabulous small college campus. I really needed to get away from West Vancouver where I felt labeled.

I was quite a good skier and was offered a scholarship to Wenatchee Valley College, WA to race on their ski team. It was apparent I would be faced with the same problems that travel, dorms, young men and women sharing close quarters created. The coach called me in and said how much they wanted me to compete. I tried to explain, and of course, no one really could grasp what my enemas entailed. I just said to him, "I am sorry, I can't travel." I knew that would be too much of a challenge and with silent tears and anger I left ski racing.

However, I had been teaching skiing since I was 15, and as a ski instructor; the pay was good, the lineups for the chair lift were nonexistent as long as I was wearing the Mission Ridge Ski School jacket. I could stay in town, stay in my own place, and take care of my physical challenges in my own time. Oh yes, and the male instructors were--hot! I could ski with anyone anywhere, and so I made friends quickly.

I had already had five years as a successful ski instructor. At sixteen while working at Grouse Mountain, I was one of the youngest to pass the Canadian Associate exam. Once I arrived in Washington to teach at Mission Ridge, they insisted I take the US first year instructor equivalent exam in order to satisfy their requirements.

After the first quarter at college, my academic past was catching up with me. I really did not have great study skills. The school notified me I would have to drop out, if I did not bring up my marks. The really amazing, thing about that time! I met my future husband that first day on campus.

I signed up for the next quarter in classes that simply looked interesting, including French which I had failed in high school. However I still enjoyed it, thanks to my Dad. My confidence was growing, and I was studying and learning differently. Being able to take classes I enjoyed was a turning point. I was getting somewhere! I made the Dean's List at the end of the term, and much of the credit goes to my study coach . . .and then fiancé, now my husband of 42 years. So how about that from probation to the Dean's List! Halleluiah! I was on a new path. I was now a good student. Who would have thought? I could see a degree somewhere in my future. I was proving to myself I had worth and value to society.

Dorm Life 1969

I really did not think about the shock I would go through with figuring out bathrooms. I had just arrived home from my trip to Europe and had adjusted on that trip as best I could. I was looking forward to leaving my home and safe nest again.

Mom was really hovering before she left me to drive back to Vancouver. Yes, she had a good reason to be worried. I really had no private place to take an enema in these dormitories. My priorities were to move out of our family home and fly little birdie, fly and live life.

I walked down the hall from our little dorm room to check out the 'can.' Oh, my, what am I going to do? There was no lock on the door, four toilets with curtains between that did not go all the way to the floor. There was only one little sink. No place to hang up my water bag, except the curtain hangers that were about 8 feet above the floor. That was just not going to work for me.

I really needed my enema. I had gone two days without it and felt sick. I stood there, and then walked back to the room. My roommate was unpacking and took one look at me and asked if I was okay? I lied and said, "I'm fine." I sat down on my hot pink side of the room to think. I was not used to asking for help. I needed to think, and I had to do something. I had to ask for help. What kind of help was I looking for and from whom?

So I went downstairs to the dorm mother. I knocked on her door. She came to the door and was very friendly. I asked if I could come in and tell her my dilemma.

She said, "Well, I am busy will this take long?"

She knew I was there for skiing, and I had just returned from an overseas trip. It was extremely necessary for me to tell her I needed a private bathroom, but before I could finish she kind of chuckled. I asked, "What is so funny?"

She said, "All of the girls want their own bathroom."

I said, "If you would let me finish, I will explain." So I did. She thought I was making it up.

She said, "Wow, that is a good one." She was actually really nice. I was so upset I did not push it.

My Mom had just left the dorms, and I wished I could have called her back. But no, I needed to manage this alone. I decided an hour later to go back to the dorm mother with a plan. She listened, and I asked to use her bathroom, "Say every other day." But she would not have that, and I can't say I blame her.

Fighting back tears, and frightened I went back to my room. I sat there and decided to tell my roommate what was going on. I should have gone to her in the first place. After I had told her what I needed, she started the best excuse and white lie campaign I ever witnessed. My roommate, bless her heart, would tell creative lies to keep the other girls out of the bathroom. I could hear her voice, "They are washing the floors", or "Some animal got in there and made a mess", etc. Eventually, the truth came out, "Keep out! My roommate is taking care of business!"

Bless her heart, this was above and beyond the call of friendship, and her time was needed for studying.

I made friends with nearly everyone in the dorm. I knew telling some people would be risky. After some time, the girls would just see my roommate sitting by the bathroom door, then turn and go the other way. I pounded a nail into the wall to hang my enema bag and set up my own thing. In those days, I normally only took one enema, and then got out of there only occupying the bathroom for twenty to thirty minutes. When I saw an opening of time, I would take more.

After the first two quarter terms of living there, I moved out to a basement suite with my high school friend and another girl from the dorm. Now I only had to worry about two roommates. Phew!

Central Washington University

It was then time to transfer to a bigger university. Now I had to decide what field I would go after. I needed to decide on a major and a minor. I was looking at Physical Education as my field. For some reason, I just kept taking classes in the areas of kinesiology, anatomy, physiology, fields that kept my attention. I was once again staring at a chance to choose my future! I believe studying these subjects would maybe give me some answers regarding my own health.

Luckily, I had a fiancé who believed in me. I wanted to make him proud. I was starting to feel the accomplishment and sense of pride academically. My whole life I had struggled in classes. I was learning how to organize better, study and dedicate my time more proficiently. I finished my degree earning a Bachelor's degree in Physical Education with minors in Art and Dance from Central Washington University. I did it! What really is amazing, hidden handicap and all, is that I taught school for twenty-five years. Why did I choose Physical Education? I simply wanted to teach students to appreciate their bodies and take care of theirs through the fun and joy of sports, dance, and active living.

It's 1971, I'm just married and living back in Wenatchee, commuting to Central Washington five days a week. I decided to work towards my U.S. National Ski Instructor certification. This would prove to be one of the most challenging, and rewarding tests I ever encountered. I studied the manual and physics of skiing. Our coach had us training for nearly a year prior to the exam. He was competitive and wanted his instructors to make him proud, just like a team. Of course, as our boss, we really wanted to please him. He made us ski fast, have control, perfect technique through trees, go through bumps on one leg and at times, ski blind-folded. He was preparing us to coach handicapped skiers. This was an excellent process, and we were truly prepared for the three day exam. We even had to pay 25 cents if we fell, and the money went towards a monthly party.

The Exam Days Were Here

After months of training, studying, and working my legs and mind; I was ready – I thought! Anyway, I had my bright red lipstick on and after a pep talk from our coach, we, his star team, met our examiners and started up the mountain. I remember sitting with one of my friends who threw up on the chair ride. Now that did not make me feel confident. She had been so nervous for weeks before. This little O'Leary was prepared. I was *ready*, bring it on! But what I was not ready for were these three grueling stressful days.

Standing at the top of a shoot which had huge bumps called moguls and with only one fall line to ski, the examiners looked at us all, clipboards in hand. They just wanted to see us ski. "Stay in the fall line, people," is all the head honcho announced. "Please go down in order." They requested us to go around those mountainous bumps with only a few seconds in between them.

I had gone through the order thing set by flagged poles before while in racing, but with no one in front or immediately behind me. When racing I was alone on the course, the gates, the snow, and a focused me.

How strange it was to follow people I didn't know. What I mean by this is if you are skiing with people you know, you also know what they can handle. Of course, two people in front of me bailed, falling to the side of the chute. I had to react, just like in my racing days and jump out of the way, and get back on the course. I knew I was able to just wiggle my feet with my knees, keep my upper body facing down the hill, and still get my skis to return to the fall line. Remember, there were people coming behind me. I did not want to be rammed into by four or five mostly big men. So I slalomed and jumped my way through all of this mayhem and stopped right next to the head examiner.

He said very quietly to me, "Wow, I just wanted to see how Mission Ridge instructors ski."

I answered, "That was a fun challenge". He never looked up from his clip board.

"Next," he instructed, "Please teach how to go through these bumps, teach beginner graduated length method or shorter skis, walking, wedge, stem Christie, traverse, carved short radius and long radius turns."

The next morning, we were assigned another examiner. She looked at me and said, "Ok, Patty is it?" As she looked at her clip board, "Please teach us to ski one-legged."

Of course, this was without the special pole skis that amputees use, but she just wanted an introduction and at a beginner level. Ha, the word "just" should not be there. I did that and all was well, except some of the people were all sprawled out on the little hill and laughing. I had to demonstrate a little discipline and get them back on track.

It was an awakening for the instructors from the other ski schools who did not have Gordon West as their coach, Mr. Drill Sergeant. Thanks to him our ski instructors shone and were a force to reckon with among the 16 schools that attended.

The third day was one I remember thinking that this one I could screw up. I have never been one who is good at written exams. I studied the manual so much it became a blur. When I sat down, my nausea went away. While writing it, I did feel I was nailing the questions.

Then it was time for the third day board exams with oral questions. After two days of showing off our talents on the hill, we had to sit on a chair, alone and answer many questions from a group of examiners sitting at a long table. It was my turn. I walked up the steps to the top floor of the ski school into a large room, found the chair and sat down. I would imagine at this point they could see me shaking. They asked me to solve situations, for example a job interview. I knew they were going to let me know if I had passed or not, and I was emotionally drained. After about ten questions, they asked me one more, and I replied, "I cannot stand the suspense. Do you have many more questions?" I knew I should not have done that.

But they all smiled and said, "Patty, that was our last question, and congratulations, you are now a fully certified United States National Ski Instructor."

I passed as we called it, my cert. I had enough training and knowledge to now teach new ski instructors, and I would get paid more. Also the rest of our ski school passed the exam. Quite a few other participants did not pass and were devastated. Just because one can play anything extremely well, does not mean one can annunciate, demonstrate the right lead up skills, analyze and make corrections. Yes, not everyone is cut out to be a teacher. But we passed. Hurrah!

What an extremely intense difficult exam to pass. It was like I earned a gold medal! Actually they did send me an official U.S. Flag pin with my name on it to wear anywhere. I still have that pin today. I was on cloud nine.

Just Us

I am aware in this day and age, there are so many marriages breaking up, and so many couples participating in second or third marriages, but I still believe in the institution of marriage. I want to talk about my husband and our many ways we work and enjoy staying together. We met, what seems a very long time ago in 1969. He was checking students into the dormitory, and no one could really ignore this soft talking, sweet, tall good looking man. He had organized a volleyball game that afternoon where we really first caught each other's eye. College life was fun, and we all were enjoying the fall activities: Goldfish eating, football, volleyball, classes and friends.

My Goldfish World Champion

With a tiny fish net, he reached in to a large bowl of hundreds of little goldfish, energetically and happily swimming around. Greg grabbed the little fish by the tail and raised its wiggly body over to his lips and popped it into his mouth. He swallowed and turned to his right, smiled at the girl who adored him and watched her do the same. At the start of this competition, there were about 12 entries. A few (smart) or chicken contestants dropped out. Then at 50 fish eaten, a few more students were visiting the happy bucket around the corner to get rid of the probably still alive guppies.

Now the contestant's numbers were slowly dropping. As they continued eating these little goldfish, it was obvious that the fish were swimming slower and slower around the bowl. Greg was interrupted by a heckler from the audience, and he invites this guy up to the stage to enter the competition. "I'll make you a deal! For $20 bucks, chew one goldfish, and join us at 100 goldfish swallowed." The heckler took the bet, selected his prey from the bowl, all the time turning a pale shade of green. Nervously he touched it to his lips…and took advantage of the happy bucket behind the stage!

Now, at about 200 fish devoured, everyone was out except the girl and Greg. The competition continued and they noticed that there were a limited number of goldfish remaining in the bowl and decided to amended the rules, to chew every other goldfish!

Someone from the crowd yelled out, "Hey Emry do you have a date tonight?" He yelled back, "No, but I do tomorrow night." Looking straight at me!

I almost left a bit embarrassed, "Wait, what I am doing?" This guy will do anything to raise money for charity. He had organized this fund raiser for local kids at Christmas, and his student council was raising the money to buy gifts.

The two of them reached the 350 mark, and with a twinkle in his eye dropped the 351st goldfish down his throat, and watched the competition bow out. This girl had perseverance! Not to mention a heavy crush on my future husband!

It was Greg on the stage by himself. He made his way through the goldfish swallowing ten at a time, and stopped at 411 swallowed goldfish. The previous record was two hundred and some…, Greg never did put this in the Guinness Book of World Records as the publication was no longer allowing records of eating live things.

Our first date was the next night. We enjoyed ourselves, but the goldfish crackers on top of the salad turned Greg that pale shade of green!

Head Over Heals!

We quickly fell for each other. I immediately knew this man was not offering any come on lines, but was a fabulous listener and sincere. Within four months, we were engaged and knew we would have a very long life together. We had amazing love and passion for each other. We also both came from parents who demonstrated a long marriage and dedication through the vows through sickness and health, etc. In short, we wanted what our parents had. We wanted to share family. We wanted to share fabulous life experiences, and of course, the difficult challenges as well.

I have over the years received the best part of the relationship, as he treats me like a queen with continued gentle care and understanding throughout our entire time together. He has only raised his voice to me when I don't listen, and then still says he loves me. He is my love!

We, reminisce about what we value, what we have learned, the good times and our failures together. The one consistent message shines through is our dedication to stay together, even in the tough times. An amazing gift, we still like each other and what we have accomplished in our time together. I still love to look at him and miss him when he's away, even on his two hour bike rides. We don't pass each other much even in closet or kitchen without a touch, kiss or a cute comment. We are God blessed. We have taught ourselves to continue these daily demonstrations of our love for each other.

After all these years, our three children are a major factor in tying us together. Like others, our children put us through the parent tests, curfew mishaps, alcohol experimentation, and their dating challenges which tested us as a couple. My husband is always willing to discuss the latest problems and what are the best solutions for our children and our lives. We work to develop a sense of consistency for when we met with our children about their issues. We wanted to be on common ground, together in agreement.

Now that our children are adults, we try not to dictate to them about what to do or not, and have tried to eliminate the guilt. We work at making family their safe haven. We want them to feel good about themselves. We are still growing and learning. My husband and I discuss whether we should jump in or let them be, and while we all need the occasional consult, they too must have the opportunity to learn from mistakes and grow in their own lives.

My husband has taught me something I did not learn growing up. He by example has and still to this day reminds me to listen. My husband reminds me of the importance of leaving our children alone. I have observed and learned from Greg to respond to others queries, and try to eliminate the unsolicited opinion. I have learned from him to act, not react!

The two of us have been and continue to be a good team. We are blessed as we still have a twinkle in our eye when we look at each other.

One of our tests

There was a time when we were challenged beyond what we could possibly be prepared for. My husband and I were on a trip, skiing and having some fun. I had pain prior to going, and found eating anything, having sex or taking enemas an ever increasingly difficult task. While we were in the hotel, the pain was extreme, so I knew something was very wrong. At least this pain was beyond the normal for my system functions. When we came home, I was forced to go in hospital and have this checked.

The doctors had me slated for surgery to examine my pain. Of course, I would have to wait for a bed, and this not knowing negatively, consumed our lives. We tried to function with life as usual. In fact while during an intimate time, I had to stop, as I had thoughts about these big questions: What if this is cancer? The doctor did say he was going to go in to check and see if it was the C word. What if I never would be able to make love to my husband again? Also I had the question that still reminds me of the utmost terror – How would my children handle it if they lose me? I may not get to see my children grow up. How would my husband take care of three very young children? Please God, give me strength to survive this, give my husband and me strength to do what we have to do to survive one more health test. At the time, my husband was out of work, trying to start his own business, but the financial strain combined with my latest medical issue created so much worry. I felt so terrible for adding this burden for him and my whole family. Our youngest was only just three years old. These babies still needed their mother.

This constant worry and unknown future caused me to think, goodbye to sleep and hello to the middle of the night, every night.

The surgery was once again not fun, but I just wanted to know one thing when I came out of anesthesia. My husband was there, of course, waiting for me to wake up. He told me I would be okay. He told me he loved me. I thanked God, and fell back to sleep.

It was at this stretch of time, my handsome very dark haired husband turned grey. Not a happy time for this very strong, and confident man. My husband did not really have anyone he felt he could speak to here in this city. He probably internalized everything. I guess turning grey was the physical result from the struggle and worry about me, never complaining to a single soul.

After many years of Greg travelling and my high risk operations we have learned to not take each other for granted. We have valued our time together. We have wanted our family to find a partner like we have. Someone that when the times become more than you think you can bare, you ask yourself one question: Do I love this person and what would my life be without them in my life?

Let's Talk Sex

Hey, I'm human. Not your normal road of discovery, but not knowing what my body would or could not do was in a way the best for me. Anyone that will talk or dare I say it, write about their sex life must feel like they are exposing their dirty -- if that is what they think it is -- laundry. I think of it as a lesson plan for my private, personal life. I luckily do not have any guilt about premarital sex. I needed to discover my physical limitations.

I'm a Catholic, so, of course, I was raised with all encompassing guilt. I remember a CCD teacher telling us if you sit on a boy's knee for more than 30 seconds, you are committing a mortal sin. He never seemed to instruct the guys with the same warning or fervor.

I won't say how old I was, but I had a serious boyfriend, and we spent times doing the usual exploration. To my surprise, a penis did not go into what I thought was my vagina. I was mortified; I had a built in chastity belt! I did not have a vagina!

When I went to see my doctor, I had questions of my own!

Wow, I really don't know how to go into this chapter, but with my unusual blocked-vaginal construction, it was definitely built in birth control.

I am glad I did explore. How else would I have known my limitations? How unfair would that have been to withhold sex until after a wedding, and then not be able to consummate. At least I was prepared, had time and explored this with the appropriate partner. I was in this alone, but had support. I was now setting a goal to have major surgery to correct the deformity, hopefully, with good results for my partner as well.

What a confused young woman I was when it came to my own sexuality. I had those messages of wait, it's private and a special interaction taught to me. I had been so very young when having to relax for doctors and interns in order that they could examine my private areas over and over. Touch and feel fingers in the anus and vagina and what was supposed to be my urethra.

My hidden handicap is quite rare, many young interns, young men mostly, would look at me, and I at them thinking they were so very handsome. Yet, oooh, what are they doing to me? "Relax, we need to do this."

I was very confused about allowing the examinations, or whether to stop them. These probing and at times sexual touches were not welcome, and wouldn't be for any young female or woman. The bright lights, the sterile exam rooms, at times, no other female present.

Okay, I admit, I wasn't a virgin when I got married. In my mind, I actually wasn't a virgin my entire life physically or mentally. So starting to explore sexual maneuvers was normal for me. Luckily for me, my boyfriend was just as inexperienced as I was, so it was the blind leading the blind. Thank heaven, the doctors did not remove my sexual senses and drive.

I have to tell you, this is really weird for me to write about! OK, let's keep this to just facts. I had normal sexual drives and feelings from a very young age. There was normal exploration and sometimes with a partner. As I developed through my teenage years, I was also able to enjoy the occasional touch. I had the G spot, up and running! Thanks to the surgeon in 1950 who saved this part of my system!

The doctor who performed my next surgery was the head of gynecology. I had a fiancé who was, luckily for me, willing to go through this with me. So I will say it now, he is gorgeous, sweet, and we really wanted each other!

We spoke with the doctor at great lengths. I think Mom was in on some of the discussions. The operation would have me opened up abdominally and vaginally, yet again. They had to reconstruct the urethra through a new vagina that would be all scar tissue. Scar tissue shrinks, and I had to take a month and a half to heal. I was fitted with a stuffed condom, the same size as an erected penis. I know, some women might say –Sweet!

For the first few weeks, I was raw tissue and stitches that really itched. My pubic hair was growing back in and created even more discomfort. My urethra was attached to the middle of my new vagina, like a little side pipe going up to the bladder. Every time I went the bathroom, I had to very carefully slide this penis shaped tampon out to just pee. It really hurt, every time! Now, give me a second, that really was weird, but how creative were these doctors, right?

February 9, 1971 Reprint Letter from Dr. F.E. Bryans to Central Washington University Health Center.

Re: Miss Patty O'Leary

I am writing to provide some background of information regarding Miss Patty O'Leary. This girl was born with a congenital abnormality of her genital tract and perineum. She had an operation for an imperforate anus as an infant, and underwent an exploratory laparotomy in Chicago at the age of three. The external genitals were clearly unusual, but no plastic procedure was done until she reached the time of her menarche when a large hematocolpos was drained through the vagina to the perineum. At this operation carried out in February 1963, laparotomy revealed a double uterus and a very large vagina distended with blood. The vagina was opened, and a passage created to permit the drainage of the dependent portion of the vagina. This served her well over the ensuing years. A dilatation of the vaginal opening was required in November 1967 when she began to have trouble with the passage of her menstrual secretions. In July of 1970, a procedure was done to create a more normal vagina. Following a perineorrhaphy to expose the lower end of the vagina, it was identified that she had a transverse vaginal septum, but above this was a normal vagina. The septum was excised and a Silastic mould was placed to maintain a more normal vaginal lumen. When she was last seen, the vagina had epithelial zed, and she had an essentially normal vagina at the apex of which were two cervices.

In September of 1969, she was seen by Dr. John Ankenman, a urologist, regarding her urinary tract function. He had previously examined her in 1963. Retrograde pyelograms were carried out in 1969 suggesting some blunting of the calyces. The vesical neck as such was large. There was no evidence of a trigone. The urethral orifices were lateral and proximal, especially on the right side with loss of intramural ureter suggesting reflux. BUN was 26 mgs. Percent. The urine sample taken at the time of cystoscopy showed numerous white cells and a heavy growth of E. coli from the right kidney and no growth from the left. Dr. Ankenman was anxious that she continue to have periodic urological assessment and that she be on long range chemotherapy.

End of Report

Greg and I on our wedding day! Things were looking up.

August 28th, 1971

Anyway, this went on for about two months. Obviously the pain diminished over time. Imagine my thrill when the doctor said it was all healed, and I didn't have to walk with this thing stuck up my new vagina!

So my fiancé and I had tried, and in all seriousness, it did take time. There were no orgasms, no great feelings for me, but it did help him. Then on our wedding night, the Lord said, "*Let there be joined orgasm!*", and the lights went on, the fireworks went off, and we had a real sex life.

Now I had a prescription for Premarin birth control pills.

I offer no apology to my kids or my parents. The way I look at this is sex was a reward for all of the surgery, men looking up my pipes, itchy pubic hairs growing back, nurses shaving every part of my body, etc. Yes, I like sex, and I earned the opportunity, and so did my husband. Now, we have been together 43 years. He puts up with a lot, so for the both of us, thanks to the medical community, and my families prayers.

Interrupted

This is a true story of love making interrupted. We bought a floating home in Richmond, and my hubby remodeled the upstairs, our love nest. We were sexually active, and at the same time, exhausted from our emotionally and physically challenging coaching and teaching careers. We wanted to have a baby, so we made appointments with each other for that reason. Of course, we wanted to reconnect after busy schedules.

My husband and I were upstairs in our little nest and, yes, we were practicing making a baby. I heard some scratching noises in the wall by our steps. I said, "Stop, do you hear that?" and like any man, he wanted to continue, and said, "I don't hear anything." Of course, the scratching got louder, and I said, "Come on, don't you hear *that?*"

Phew, he finally heard it and said, "I have to see what's in the wall."

Still wearing our birthday suits, we put our ears up to the wall and listened. We thought it may be a bird. Greg decided to go into our little low ceiling closet under the steps to check. Something was in behind the plywood wall. He pulled a small part away and a very large river rat jumped out over his shoulder and started to run all over the main floor. Luckily it was still light outside, and we could see this very large rat under the floor heater staring at us. I said to Greg, "At least, put hiking boots on!" He did just that. I proceeded to jump up on the coffee table with the broom in my hands.

We opened our gothic glass doors that went all the way to the floor and out to the river hoping it would just run out and escape.

The rat ran across the room and was now hiding behind our free standing fireplace glaring at us, ready to attack, it did just that. I swung the broom with all my might in a sweeping action and, of course, took out our only lamp, but not the rat. But, alas, all was quiet. Hmmm, the rat was no where in sight, and seemed to be gone. So we cleaned up the broken lamp, poured ourselves a glass of wine and sat down on our couch toasting our victory over the vermon!

Then, we heard and felt a nearby thud, and could not believe our eyes! The rat had hid in the very couch we were sitting on. It was in behind our backs. In a flash we were both back on the coffee table, and now the rat was in the kitchen stretched out under another heater. My husband went on the attack and at the same time the rat jumped out. Greg jumped up and landed on the back of his opponent. The rat was squirming and biting at Greg's boot. Greg said, "Honey look the other way." Soon the rat was dead.

We then got dressed, put the lamp back together and finished the bottle. The wine tasted especially good that night. Greg is my hero!

It takes a sense of humour! We laughed about the comedy of it all, went to bed and fell asleep in each other's arms.

Aging Issues

There have been many times when intercourse did not hurt. But, over time my system has changed. The ring of scar tissue about an inch up my vagina has become extremely sensitive, and as my Doctor informed me, shrinking. My vagina has shortened somewhat, and the vaginal wall has thinned. Also, the urethra that feeds into this column has become an area that has, at times, suffered from trauma and is prone to collecting germs from my enemas which has instigated kidney infections. Ouch! I even today take an antibiotic following each time we make love.

I am playing with the cards I was dealt, mostly I get a pair, occasionally an ace high full house. I still think my man is gorgeous and sexy, but we have to take entry slow. We have adjusted, learned to communicate and workout a routine. I enjoy holding him and love when he surrounds and envelopes my little body in his. I will always be a sexy woman to my husband, and sexy in my mind as well.

Sex is a huge thing to give away. And, even at my age today, I have decided even with a lower sex drive, pain, and history, to refuse to have my sex life hijacked. Growing up together sexually was fun, and our long relationship has been extremely sweet. We continue to make love, hold and enjoy each other; I am truly blessed.

1973 Back to Canada

June of 1973 my husband and I moved back to Vancouver as Greg had accepted a teaching/coaching position at Vancouver College. My first job was teaching at my old elementary school. The pay was horrible, but the job was a great learning experience for me. I taught P.E. and Art, was secretary of the school, and the CCD program. On top of that I coached volleyball, as well as track and field. After one year I was offered another teaching job at a girl's high school across the city. I was being recognized for my achievements.

I cognitively decided I was going to make the best of this career, and teach students the appreciation of sport and of their body. Thus my views led me to influence young women, and I taught my entire career in private all girl schools. Physical Education found me, so I found myself. This is what I was put on this earth to accomplish. I decided to live my life to its potential. I decided to say, 'Yes', to get more in return.

Early in my career, I was asked to be a Department Head and Athletic Director. Both positions challenged me to grow within my chosen career. I also enjoyed creating lifestyle programs for obese children and their parents within our school setting. I volunteered for the BCSSGVA committee and learned much from experienced intelligent women. I was asked to serve on that board and had to rise to the occasion. Once again, I was entering challenges academically I never thought possible. People were looking to me for leadership.

I have tried to stay fit, set simple goals to get up in the morning, and try to not complain every waking moment. I have always wanted to prove to myself and others that my body succeeded even though there are those parts that have let me down.

Being a positive individual attracts the same. I learned to market myself as someone others would like to be around, and move forward knowing I have a support system.

Travel with My Husband

Most importantly, while traveling with my husband, I often would be 'poisoned' from my system backing up, caused by the change of diet, time zones, lack of regular exercise and sleeping in different beds, my system just has a difficult time adjusting to change.

1978 Island of Sciathos, Greece, Greg and Mary Anne P.

In 1978 my husband and I decided to spend the summer in Europe, backpacking and staying in B and B's. Several times in the middle of the night, I became very ill, poisoned by my own system, and Greg would wake up to my petit mal seizures. I would feel dizzy, light headed and faint. I needed to lie down and have it all stop, just asking him to hold me. He didn't know what to do, nor did I at the time. I still today am extremely frightened, and years later I at least have some faith that the Gravol will kick in to save me!

I am really not worth anything after these bad poisonings, I basically need to sleep and rest because they were so very hard on me. We have cancelled flights and vacations at the last minute because my stomach was rumbling, or due to feeling faint, ill, or like I was going to have diarrhea. Frankly, I would welcome diarrhea, at least, things would come out and the contaminated stool would be gone.

Three Blessings

1981 - Our First Born

Yes, I have practiced my whole life to change an uncontrollable situation into something good. Adoption was luckily a way to change numerous surgeries into a true blessing.

My husband and I tried to get pregnant after seven years of marriage. After a consult with my doctor, he felt that pregnancy would potentially be dangerous, not only to me, but likely I would not be able to carry full term. In fact at this time, he mentioned I may have miscarried a few times over the past few years. So my husband and I needed to turn our family plan, our life towards realistic choices.

We started talking about adoption. Once convinced the pregnancy wouldn't be a good thing to go through with my health, we really started to think about it more seriously. I felt tremendous guilt that I was not going to be able to give Greg our baby. We heard how difficult adoption could be. The trend was for women who initially intend to give a child up for adoption was to change their minds at the last minute, or a grandparent would take the infant.

We finally agreed to adopt. We decided to move on, knowing and satisfied this was destiny. It will be glorious. We understood it would be a long process and an emotional rollercoaster. We had gone through mourning if you will for about five years. We were sad and jealous when friends got pregnant, especially when it was so quick for them. I don't know about Greg, but I was also angry as I noticed more and more people with new babies. It seemed our friends would talk about having a baby, shake hands with their significant other, and 'ta da' they were expecting. I got so I did not want to hear them tell me, and it took all of my will power to be supportive for them. Jealousy is a nasty emotion.

We finally one day picked up the phone and made an appointment. However, we really had no idea how many ups and downs we would face. The family study is the first step of the adoption process. Our social worker and her superiors asked my husband and me numerous questions. Our friends and family members were quizzed:

Did we argue? How did we make up? What did we do for holidays? What did we do for a living? Did we abuse alcohol? What were our likes and dislikes? Our employers were also asked to fill out a questionnaire. It was obvious they would not give new babies up for adoption to just anyone.

The process was thorough and thoughtful in order for the birth mother to possess enough information to find the perfect family for her child.

We were accepted, and became one of approximately four hundred plus "case studies" or potential adoptive couples. Our social worker then attempts to match our case study to a potential relinquishing woman or couple. Two to three case studies at a time are provided to the birth mother, and she decides the most suitable home for the adoptive child. No doubt a very difficult decision for any one, let alone a young mother. I believe these are strong woman and had support to guide them along the way.

The Waiting Process

More than two years into the wait, we already had two false calls. God has his plan, and we needed to trust in it. My husband and I would tell each other, "Hey, who wouldn't choose us?" Our social worker told us sometimes the birth mother chooses based on whether the potential parents have a golden lab, or a pet monkey --- seriously!

We did have the first "almost" call. The social worker phoned and said a birth mother was looking at our case study. Then we got a call, and we were short-listed. Then we got another call, and the birth mother chose another set of parents for her child. That was a tough time. We became quiet for a few weeks, each of us in our own deep thoughts.

The second opportunity was even more difficult. We had planned a vacation to the Oregon coast, when we received notice that we were once again short-listed. No cell phones in 1980, but we were asked to phone every few hours. Away we go, down Interstate 5, constantly questioning what we should do, turn around or continue our trip? We phoned from every rest stop, and still no news, so we turned around. We kept telling ourselves, trust in God's plan. Trust in the plan, again and again.

I had been fortunate enough to attend university, graduated and teach in my chosen field. I was good at my job as head track and field and volleyball coach, AD - athletic director, Phys Ed department head. My teams kept me working early mornings and late nights. My husband traveled fifty percent of the time in his sales and marketing job, and coached for a local track club. Needless to say, we were having fun and working ridiculous hours. We were so busy we were able to keep our minds somewhat off the waiting game that was now into the fourth year, after ten years of marriage.

At work I arranged a meeting with my school principal to review the adoption process and post-adoption plan, and it was decided to wait and see. She agreed to support me.

Life was really good, and we had just moved into a nice three bedroom rancher, secretly hoping it would help move the adoption process along. We had lived on the Fraser River in a floating home, and believed our adoption chances improved if we changed our living arrangements. We were right. Three months after we moved into our new home, away from all of that water, we were rewarded.

It was mid-March 1981, and my husband was away at work in Seattle, and I was home doing dishes when the phone rang. It was our social worker. She asked "Can you and Greg take the day off tomorrow and meet me at the hospital at 11 am to pick up your new little girl?"

Oh, my God, those words---Ahhh, I am now crying, "Give me a moment!"

I immediately phoned my husband. At first, Greg was not to be found in the Seattle hotel. I was able to contact his business associate and let him in on what was happening so he would urgently look for him. Greg was pulled out of a meeting and came to the phone, and I could hardly get the words out, I was crying and laughing all at the same time. He said he was leaving Seattle as soon as he got packed. My next call was to my parents.

Wow, I almost forgot that day's emotions! Was this really happening? "I am going to be a mother tomorrow!" Did we have nine months to prepare? Was a room ready?

My inner voices were running wild with huge questions and decisions that needed to be made. I need to tell my workplace, but maybe I shouldn't, and of course Day Care?! Oh my goodness!

Luckily, I could once again get my mother's assistance. She came over, and we raced to "The Bay" where we bought a crib, baby clothes, formula, bottles, and oh yes---diapers. We gutted and cleaned the intended baby's room, and readied it for our new arrival. I kept questioning, "How are we going to adjust? This is happening so very fast?" Yes, after four years, it is still an instant surprise to new parents, just as each life birth startles us!

Reality- The 30 Day Trial

All adoptions in British Columbia are regulated by the government. The birth mother's consent for the adoption is not taken until, at least, ten days after the birth of the child. In addition, and here is the worry point for adopting parents, the birth mother may withdraw her consent to the adoption within thirty days of the child's birth. In other words, once we accepted the baby, it was not totally carved in stone that we would be able to keep the baby. We could hold and fall in love with the baby, and then have to hand her back to the birth mother. Can you imagine? It's all part of the deal! It really takes a sense of humour!

It would be heart breaking. However, we respected any woman that was so loving and generous to think about giving up their biological baby to total strangers. Also what she must have gone through to get to that point?

My husband arrived home with the biggest grin and tears in his eyes. He was holding a little red dress for the baby. We had a good chuckle; it was for a two year old. He was too excited to know, or how to ask for the right size in the store. The next morning, we gathered our wits about us and started our drive to get our new bundle of joy.

We double checked with our social worker about the time we were to meet her at the hospital and arrived early. In the lobby, very nervous, extremely anxious, but trying to be confident, always with the fear the biological mother may change her mind at the last moment, then we met our social worker. She proceeded to list the *do's and don'ts* while at the hospital.

The instructions when we meet the nurses who worked with the biological mother were:

1. Do not say where you live.

2. Do not say your names.

3. Do not say where you or family members work.

4. Do not say what you do for a living.

5. Do not call each other by name.

6. Do not ask about the birth mother.

Off we went, an excited couple who have waited for a long time for this day, nearly four years!

At the top of the stairs, holding hands and trying to look "cool", our social worker met us and said, "OK, the nurse will bring the baby to the big window, and the two of you can look to see if you still want the baby?"

The nurse brings this little miracle bundle to the window, she is swaddled, tied and her swollen little red face peaked out. This little baby's face was so swollen that her eyes looked like she was an Asian infant. I looked at her through the window, and I said, "I don't know what to do!" The social worker said, "If you have changed your mind that's okay?"

I said, "Oh, no! I want that baby, and want her now! I just don't know what to do with her red face!"

One nurse then led us into the nursery to change and feed the baby. It was a little awkward knowing that the nurses potentially had an emotional attachment and knew the birth mother. Our hearts were beating out of our chests. We looked at each other in disbelief and sheer excitement. Our strong emotions felt incredible then looking at her through the window was also incredible, but now to be able to hold her, words cannot express the joy! We wanted to sing Hallelujah!

We laid our new child snuggled in a blanket in an infant wash tub on the floor of the

front passenger seat. We were on our way home, and a car runs a red light, barely missing us. Our attention was immediately focused on our new baby, and a very new feeling of care and protection for our new little stranger laying quietly on the floor in the baby tub between my feet. She already had trust in her eyes as she looked up at my face.

I remember saying a few prayers that day for so many reasons.

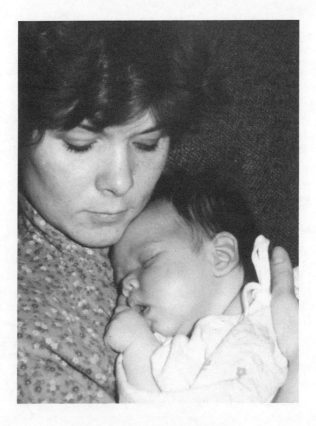

Erinn at Two Months

The very first night home, both emotionally exhausted, we faced our first night of feedings every two hours. We really had no idea what we were in for, apart from the Adoption Orientation classes taken three years earlier.

Greg said naively, "I'll take the first feeding tonight."

We heard her little cry, and at first coming from a deep sleep, we both thought, "What is that?"

Greg rolled over and said, "I'll get it tomorrow night."

Yes, I thought, "As if that would happen!" I was wrong, he was great. He was up many nights with her, and I knew this man was dedicated. We both learned that even though we were not nursing her, bottle feedings were a healthy thing for both parents to have that one-on-one bonding time. It was very satisfying to hold her, watching her every move, listening to that quiet sucking on the bottle and her gentle breathing.

Social Worker from Heaven

Many baby showers were given for our new family. We were having so much fun with our new addition, Erinn. But always in the back of our minds was the looming thought that the birth mother still had to sign the final release to finalize the adoption, to make Erinn legally ours. After counting down the nineteen days, we received a call from our social worker. Our entire family and all of our friends kept calling us daily to find out the verdict. It drove us crazy. "We'll let you all know when we know." The news was that our social worker wanted to come over, and deliver the final papers. She walked into our home and said, "It's final! You're her parents!" Thank God, and God bless that young birth mother for her demonstration of true trust and love.

Work

The school had a fundraiser, so I had a few days off of work to get organized. We got the news, and I needed time. This school bazaar gave me a chance to find babysitting or daycare. Greg and I were calling all over the city asking friends and family to take her for three different days of the week. My parents lived across the city, and Mom agreed to take her two days a week. Another friend took her one day a week.

I was in the middle of coaching a club volleyball team, and head high school track and field team, plus my regular teaching responsibilities. Initially I took Erinn to the practices and managed the activities while she was in her stroller. Three activities to manage, and interrupted sleep from 'my thing', plus our new baby to care for was a trying time. In short, I was overwhelmed, and I soon found that having a career and motherhood is not "Having it all!" I would *not* be able work fulltime.

Prior to the adoption, I had met with the Sister Superior of the Catholic girl's school where I taught. At the time, we discussed supporting my activities by hiring substitutes, allowing me to work half time for the remainder of the school year.

I also believed that I would be able to work half time in the next school year. They will help me, right? Not so! At the time neither the school, nor the Ministry of Human Resources, were supportive of new fulltime 'working' mothers.

I remember vividly a day at the shopping mall leisurely walking along with our baby, enjoying the moment, realizing at this point my job can wait. I needed and wanted to take care of this child. I spoke with Sister Superior and resigned my teaching/coaching position. Later, however, we found this to be a very unrealistic financial situation.

Messy Art Work

When as a new mother, we all think we will be able to do a perfect job. You are when you do the best you can. Here is my reality – shit happens, literally.

My daughter was about 14 months old and in her crib. I came down the hall to hear some cut little jabber going on in her room. She was content and happy as only a loved, cuddled and well taken care of child does. But what the? I was gagging in the hall! What was that smell? Holy smokes! I walked into her room and gasped. She had a huge smile on her face. She had dug into her diaper and was creating her own mural with her stuff – you know her stuff. It was in her hair, on the crib, like I said all-- over the wall.

I ran and opened the window as wide as I could. Still she was happy, calling out Ma Ma. I did not grab her at first, but I went in to fill the bathtub to get that ready. At that point I must admit, I broke out laughing. What do I grab first? Do I start to wipe the walls and crib so it won't dry up or do I get her? Of course, I chose her. I held her straight armed out away from my body, and she and I were giggling down the hall towards the bathroom. I had just changed her diaper about an hour before, and it was like she enjoyed my surprise. Needless to say I was thinking just clean her up, then Lysol the whole house. Once I put her in bed for the night, I poured myself a deserving glass of wine

This was one of the tests of motherhood and how one would handle it. All I can say is this child was very easy to potty train. Now that she is a mother, she is very patient when she has to change her little guy's diaper.

Art Work and A Bath!

I had put Erinn, two years old at the time, in her play pen for a nap. After my first attempt at 'my thing', I went to check on her and found her gone. She had climbed out and was on our back porch completing an art project on my parent's Golden Lab, Shannon! She had taken a black permanent marker and was just giving the finishing touches to her work of art on the dog. An 'X' on Shannon's forehead and stripes adorned her back.

Erinn Christine – Captain of her ship. She was empowered!

We had been taking care of the dog and were to return her to Mom and Dad the next day. So, of course, I reacted and said to her, "Oh no, now we will have to give the dog a bath and wash her."

Her art activity was happening while I was still in the middle of my enema, so I made certain she was safely back in her play pen, before I went back to continue 'my thing'. She was jabbering away, and once again that suspicious silence. I came out to see her on the back porch with the rest of her lunch that I had left on the kitchen table. She was giving the dog a bath with the bright red sauce of spaghetti and meat balls. She saw me and said, "Shannon, bath!" With a big smile on her face, she was so very proud of herself.

What could I say? The best part of this was the dog was taking care of her. Ahhh, Labs are the best dog, most gentle and of course, the dog loved the massage, and licking the sauce off of her paws. It takes a sense of humour!

We quickly learned our lives would never be the same, and would be awesome forever. We had no idea how lucky we were at the time, but certainly do now. Thirty two years later, our daughter and son-in-law have a new little boy. Our first grandchild!

This was a time in my life when I started running, and training for the marathons. I surrounded myself with fit, intelligent, and empowered women.

Patty front row (right) kneeling

1984 Our Second Gift

Parenting Erinn was exhausting, and at the same time, so much fun. Being the first, I never really knew what to expect. We waited about a year before we put our names in to adopt a second child. We were ready to go through the process again, wanting our family to grow, and a sibling for Erinn.

We were finding not many people understood what it was like to adopt. Some people said the dumbest things to us, "Can you love a child that is not yours?" or "Don't you want the baby to look like you?", I wish we could all just walk in other's shoes. I am just amazed at how some people do not have a filter. Occasionally people would say, "You got off easy. You did not have to go through pregnancy or the delivery!"

Adoption is exhausting, the waiting game, the emotion, and it wears on your mental health with the long wait. The disappointment of being 'short listed' without success is very trying on the spirit. Furthermore, we were warned that few birth mothers relinquish a child to a couple that already has a baby.

In 1984, we were still waiting for our second adoption to go through, when my husband lost his job due to the economic downturn Wow, not what we expected. The two of us were going to have to find something to pay the bills on our own. While seeing 'head hunters' and interviewing for a new career, my husband did everything to help around the house. He started his own sales and marketing business, and even trimmed hedges and cut lawns for a landscape company.

Guess what! The phone call came for our next adoption. Our social worker said, with great excitement in her voice "How would you like a son? Can you pick him up the next day in northern BC?"

We packed our little three year old up and did the thirteen hour drive. Our daughter Erinn kept asking the question, "Are we there yet?" We kept reminding her that it's a long way to where her brother was born, and we all need to be patient. She would nap and then when she would wake with the same question, "Are we there yet?" Every parent knows this line.

We arrived on a grey overcast day, and drove directly to the hospital as instructed by our social worker. Even to this day, my husband and I have no memories of the hospital, other than we were there for such a very short time. I guess they really did their research on us. We received their congratulations, and they handed him over to us.

I remember later that evening having our little blond blue-eyed eleven day old baby boy in our arms. At one point his very proud big sister held him for us, and he looked up to her and smiled.

The next morning, my husband and I looked at each other, gave a little smile and said, "Wow, here we go!"

We are now a complete family of four with a beautiful daughter and son. Never in our wildest dreams did we expect to fall in love with this little guy so quickly too. What an amazing process we had gone through. We were told a social worker would pop by any time in the near future to see how we were all doing.

The next morning, we left and drove the 13 hours back to Vancouver. This time we had another pair of hands to hold his bottle, talk with him and give us reports every few seconds. A very good big sister!

We were glad the social worker did not ask us about our careers. She came to our home to check on us and to our surprise she really did not even want to see the babies.

The children were asleep, so I asked, "Don't you want to see them"?

She answered, "No, I am just checking to see how you are doing? The house looks clean; you look relaxed and happy." Obviously we passed all of her tests. With our little Kevin, we now had a complete family! Wow!

Child Explorer

Up at the summer cabin on the Sunshine Coast of BC where we are surrounded by water, I slip away during knap time to do 'my thing.'

Kevin Danal

When I came out, two of the three chitlins were accounted for, but "Where was Kevin?" Mom thought he was on the front porch or playing in the fenced yard. The front gate was closed. However, the bottom of it could be pushed out, and our little mechanically-minded soul could slip sideways through it. Of course, he is no where to be found. Kevin was my explorer and very early on an expert at curiosity, and I love him for it.

I asked my Mom, "Where is he?"

Immediately we both looked at each other, then we started to furiously look all around the cabin. We started to ask neighbors to look and were calling his name. Total panic set in. I directed neighbors to run to the nearest three beaches. I mean, I was beside myself. I was frozen in my tracks as he was not answering our calls. The ocean's tide was low, and if you walk far enough out across the sand and water, there is a point where it drops into very deep water.

A neighbor saw a child wearing a red cap way out on the rocks around the corner toward the next bay, but it wasn't him. Everyone was running and yelling. This is a remote island, no cell phones, no police, just us. Mom kept saying just pray. Ok, prayers are excellent, but of course, I kept asking, "Where is he?"

Then off in the distance – towards the fourth beach – someone yells, "Isn't that your husband with Kevin?"

My husband had been innocently sitting on our front beach reading, and thought we sent Kevin down to him. So then everyone gave my poor hubby h---! I just thanked Mom and God for the prayers. Obviously, this little boy did his usual. 'Hey I think I can get out of this yard and go spend time with my Dad,' and, so he did. OMG, right?

Escape # what? I don't know, he was the master of escape and curiosity!

Kevin's Empowerment!

My sister's family had just finished their annual visit with us at the cabin. My brother-in-law and sister were packing up their children to leave when Brenty said innocently to Kevin, now six years old, "Do you want to go get the boat?"

Minutes later Brent leaves, and walks over to the other bay to get the large family boat. On arrival, he notices the boat is not there. He even looks deep in the water to check to see if it had sank. Had it been stolen? He looks up to see just the back end of the boat going around the corner into the bigger bay where we all live. The poor guy would rather be on skates than run, but he booted it back towards our beach.

Meanwhile, we were bringing gear to the beach, it's mid-tide. The boat is approaching the beach in water about three feet in depth. In large boats like this the leg and propeller are lifted electro-mechanically so not to drag in the sand. People on the beach and I are watching, but we can't see Brent. All we see is a little blond head looking up over the steering wheel. The engine leg comes up properly, and we assume Brent is pulling a fast one on us. I look up at the cliff and see my anxious brother-in-law sprinting through the sand towards us, looking like he is going to kill someone. We glance back to the boat, and Kevin jumps up on the bow alone, throws out the anchor, and perfectly slides the boat up to the water's edge slowly and in control.

People sitting on the beach were impressed, I wasn't. I was flabbergasted and concerned about my brother-in-law. I love this man and respect him. I said to him only this, "Brent take Kevin to the cabin and remember this, finish with you love him."

That afternoon we phoned my parents as it's their boat. My mother guessed "That shows you how smart this little boy is!" She called for my dad to come to the phone. He only said, "Kevin, we love you and never, I repeat, never do anything like that in a car."

We reminded Kevin of the dangers, insurance and of the potential liabilities. We also reminded Brent, "Never ask a child, Do you want to go get the boat?" Ask, "Do you want to go with me?" Okay, at least, when one is talking with Kevin. I note that Kevin had never driven such a big boat, only through observation did he pick up on everything required to operate it: activating the engine blower, turning on the battery, untying the boat from the cleats, bring in the bumpers, maneuver the boat away from the tight dock, other boats and watch out for the water skiers, etc. He had only seen the progression watching the adults in the past, and he certainly was a quick learner!

1986 A Miracle – An Operation I Actually Looked Forward To!

This operation was much anticipated, and we were excited. I was going to have a baby.

Surprise-Surprise-Surprise!

A surprise to everyone, especially the doctors! We were warned at the adoption orientation classes of the high percentage, nearly seventy percent of adoptive parents have their own biological child after they adopt. Greg and I had tried for so very long before we adopted. I had been off birth control for, at least eight years. Considering my health history, coupled with ten years of trying to conceive, we came to assume we were not going to be part of those statistics. We were merrily going along enjoying the two precious little people in our lives.

My younger sister Teresa was getting married around the same time, I was training for another marathon, and my period was late. Friends started teasing me, "Hey, you look pregnant!"

My older brother, now a Doctor asked, "Hey, your hips look wider, are you certain you're not pregnant?"

I admit I seemed to be extremely tired, but was enjoying my sister's pre-wedding parties, and having family around. My husband and I bought an in home pregnancy test, it turned color right away! OMG!

My first sign of this pregnancy was the unending fatigue. I felt really excited, thus positive about this baby.

I was constantly aware of how at risk both my baby and I were, and at the same time, truly believed there was a reason I was with this child. I could not be happier. At least with this child, my family and I were able to know when this baby would be born. Definitely a different stress this time, but knowing the time line was really helpful.

At three months, I only had morning sickness on two occasions. Once was on my birthday. We were traveling across a busy bridge with no place to stop; I reached into the back seat and grabbed a bag gracefully, but quickly relieving myself. I was still running and teaching fitness classes. All seemed to be going really well. Amazing!

The fact that I am a small woman also meant I started to feel this very hard bump forming in my stomach. I always tried to hold my stomach in, so this was a little strange for me.

I was still able to wear some of my workout clothes, and really didn't experience any negative feelings about my increasing weight or size. In fact around the fourth month, I was playing with my two children and was stopped in my tracks with a little flutter in my stomach as if a butterfly was flying around. This was really exciting for our little clan.

Of course, I noticed my breasts were now growing, and I was not used to this. Athletic women, who do cardio as much as I do, definitely don't carry body fat in that area. I found it awkward and cumbersome. It was a good lesson for me as later when I coached athletes with larger breasts, I had a much better understanding of what they were going through.

I admit I was not one to wear a bra very often. Especially with all of the running, a rubbing bra would create a rash on my skin. I have never been comfortable wearing a bra during an enema due to the pressure it adds on my stomach. I was now really starting to require a bra, so off I went to the mall to shop. Huh, that was an experience!

I started to look for bra's and maternity clothes. That was really discouraging, ugly stuff was all I could find. Soon, I will actually need to get these clothes, and one day I will look pregnant, not just fat. I really thought about buying one of those T-shirts that have the arrow pointing down to the tummy that says 'Under Construction'. Mom thought that was a terrible idea, and was probably right, again.

At five months, Mom luckily found two really cute outfits. In fact, later I had friends borrow them for their pregnancies. My mother-in-law sent me what I call the Mrs. Cleaver tops, you know, the plaid top with the big bow at the neck. Sorry, Mama E, I used it, but only around the house. Seriously, there was generally not much available, and the outfits were expensive. So like many expectant mothers, I really only liked four tops and wore them for five long months.

Around the sixth month my belly was pretty big and I thought, "How can I possibly get any bigger?" My back would ache when I had to pick up my little thirteen month old child.

During an enema I was concerned about the space available for the baby. I knew I had a double uterus, and we all were wondering "How would this work, and what impact will it have? Would this child come out early due to the limited space? Would my little "it" have nutrition problems?"

It was at this period of time when I was taking an enema, the baby would move all over the place and kick like hell. There was really no advice being offered from my wonderful doctors. I was just winging it! I was sent to another specialist for the pregnancy, a new doctor who was going to join in with Dr. Fred Bryans, Dr. Carpenter and my anesthesiologist, his name was Dr. Gambling. Interesting names, eh what? I arrived at Dr. Carpenter's office hoping to get more guidance, but mostly he was there and talking to me about uteruses, C section, and my baby's health. I had numerous ultra sounds to make certain this cute *little munchkin* was growing all of its parts. A date was set for the C section, and I was informed about Braxton Hicks, sleeping skills, and that was it.

I was getting huge. My dear husband took me out to buy a new dress to go out to a party. A white knit dress. I looked like a big snow ball, as wide as I am tall. I sat on the edge of the bed and told him I am too fat, and he, of course, replied which didn't help, "No, honey, you are just pregnant!" The poor guy, he couldn't have said anything that I would have liked to have heard. On a brighter side, I was given so much love from this very excited man.

I was working out, still trying to run, slowly every day. I would take my two children to day care, then for 1 ½ hours hang out with adults, walking, running and strength training, the best idea ever. At 7 months I was starting to feel the pressure of the baby down low, and the jogging became a little more challenging. I only kept it up for another week or two. I really wanted to be fit for this birth. What if I went into early labor? I wanted to be strong. I must say, this baby kicked, punched, rolled, danced and bobbed its head.

At eight months, I started getting Braxton Hicks contractions quite often. I joked, "Look, I have a shelf to put my cup of tea, a little crumb catcher." So much fun! My breasts were huge. The plan was to nurse this child. Why not? I wanted to experience as much of this as I could.

In my husband's family, only two baby girls were born in three generations, and I felt this baby may be a boy. We decided to not be informed of our baby's sex; we wanted that to be a surprise.

Delivery Day

My in-laws came up from Olympia, Washington to be here for the birth. They took care of our two oldest children during my time in the hospital. Our daughter was now in playschool, and our son was only 16 months, active and as curious as can be. Our daughter knew what was happening and was so excited. The whole clan was waiting with great anticipation. What was this baby going to be? How would I deal with the delivery? And most importantly, with my history, 'Would the baby turn out with all ten fingers and toes?'

My husband was amazing and calm. Emotionally, he said "We have a little boy! I love you!" Now doesn't that say it all!

I got to see the baby, "Whew, what is all of that white stuff on his face?" "Who cares, he's gorgeous!"

After the baby was delivered, and before I was closed up, the doctors performed an examination on my very different and interesting inside tract.

Then I was moved me into a recovery room, my parents and my in-laws came to see their new grandson and me. The nurse wanted me to nurse our son right there. I was not feeling so hot, nauseous, but once again, "Okay, let's do this!"

Mom was so very nervous with worry about me. She was really quiet as she looked at the newborn, and said, "Oh, he looks like a little monkey." What!

He was an early birth so was a little wrinkled, so maybe he looked like a cute little monkey. Of course, I was just thrilled he was nursing, and looked like he had all of his parts and exits. He did not inherit my problems. Thank God for little miracles!

April 23, 1986 Grace Hospital Dr. C. Carpenter Pregnancy, 38 ½ -39 weeks with maternal genital tract anomalies/Low Transverse Caesarean Section

Under the epidural anesthetic the patient was prepped and draped and the catheter was placed into the bladder. Considerable difficulty was encountered in placing the catheter as the urethral opening was on the posterior surface of the symphysis and high up in the anterior vaginal wall. However, with curved forceps we were able to direct the tip in and gained satisfactory entry.

The patient was prepped, draped and had received an epidural anesthetic by Dr. Gambling.

Good anesthesia was obtained. A transverse lower abdominal incision was made two finger breadths above the symphysis and over the head of the baby which was easily palpable underneath.

The recti were separated and it was noted that the bladder ran high so that we entered into the peritoneal cavity relatively high. The bladder was reflected downwards but the separation was poor. The left horn could be felt, was enlarged, soft and in a lateral position not anterior as previously noted early in the pregnancy but in its typical lateral position.

The incision was made into the uterine wall and deepened. There was a fairly thick wall in this area. It was spread laterally by blunt dissection.

By fundal pressure and upward deflection of the head was delivered.

A healthy baby boy was delivered, breathed and cried spontaneously and was resuscitated by Dr. Bob MacLean. Apgars were given of 9 and 9 and I understand the weight is 2860.

The placenta delivered spontaneously. We inspected the pelvis and noted that the left horn of the uterus did not actually communicate with the vagina as we did not note it, nor did it appear to have a separate opening into the right uterine mass. Inspection of the distal part of that tube showed that the left tube disappeared in a mass of adhesions over the bowel and the ovary was not visible, nor indeed entirely palpable but the proximal part of the left round ligament and fallopian tubes were clearly visualized.

On the right side the tube and ovary appeared normal and there was a small fibroid in the anterior wall of the uterus otherwise it appeared essentially clear.

The uterus was repaired in three layers using chromic in catgut in the first two layers and 00 chromic over the peritoneum. Good hemostasis was achieved. Good reapproximation of the uterus was achieved.

The abdomen was then closed in layers using chromic in the peritoneum, Dexon continuous an uninterrupted in the fascia, subcuticular 00 Dexon in the fascia and staples and Steri-Strips in the skin.

It should be noted that the amniotic fluid was clear and bright as it surrounded the baby.

At the end of the procedure the patient was in good condition and returned to the P.A.R.

End of Report

—

June 30, 1986 print Letter Dr. C. Carpenter to Dr. P.C. Quelch Re: Patty Emry

Just a note regarding Patty Emry who attended for a postpartum visit on June 26, 1986. The baby is doing fine and seems to be a healthy husky little fellow.

She continues to have some spotting and bleeding which is relatively a long period of time; and it is now two months since her delivery.

Birth Control is via plans for Greg's' vasectomy.

Physical Examination- She appeared well. The blood pressure was normal at 120/80. The incision was well-healed and free of edema. The pelvic showed the restructured external genitalia. There was still some vaginal bleeding. The uterus itself was anteverted, bulky and of normal size. There was no swelling. The adnexal areas felt clear.

Impression- was that of a normal status although the bleeding seemed prolonged and it is possible that it was coming from the secondary uterine cavity.

I was unable to complete a pap smear so she is going to return in three months for a follow-up.

Once again, many thanks for your kind referral. End of Report

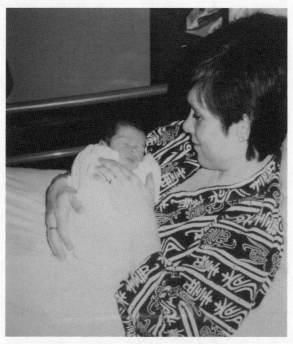

Shea Christopher and Patty

As a side note, I nursed and found it, let's just say interesting. I was glad when the four months had gone by, and I could start with the bottles and share the feedings. Although a wonderful experience for the bonding, I believe I would have done that anyway. Mostly, I was trying to take care of two other young children and was exhausted all of the time. I really don't know how people nurse for years? My oh my, it's not for me. I wanted my small athletic breasts back.

It was time to not have this child attached to me any longer. I told my husband, "I love him, but I carried him for nine months, and I still have to carry our other son Kevin."

My back needed a rest, and at the fourth month I stopped nursing, that was long enough. I admit, nursing was extremely handy at the cabin though. No microwave up there. The plan now for me was to give my body a break. It was time to get back into shape and run again. Also, I had three little ones to join me in my daily dance with the jolly jumpers, and walks with the stroller. We were living life.

#3 Baby Boy

Our youngest child is healthy. We were concerned he may get some of the family ailments passed down. However, when younger he did suffer from asthma. Even with the slightest cold, he would get ear infections and was placed on antibiotics often. I remember he often looked like he was struggling to breathe.

My mother is the one that pointed it out to me. I guess like everyone I just wanted my babies to be healthy and not have any health issues whatsoever.

Shea Christopher – piggy back!

On one occasion while my husband was away for one of his many three week trips overseas, I had to neglect him. I could not go to him. Shea was just a toddler, and while I was in the bathroom struggling with my enema, not feeling at all well, and I really needed to just stay there. Shea came to the door of the bathroom and was calling for me.

It was bed time, and I thought he was asleep in his crib. He was pretty athletic at that young age, had climbed out, came down the steep stairs, and just wanted to cuddle. I had to talk with him through the door, but he kept calling me, wanting to come in. Needless to say this was emotionally difficult.

If I pick him up, I likely will have an accident with my bowels right there. If I walk with him back up the stairs, more of a chance an accident will happen, a quandary? Just before I came out, it became very quiet. Every parent knows that usually means he could be into something he should not be or he has fallen asleep. When I came out, there he was on the floor, lying right by the door, asleep. Whew, I dodged that one.

He did this again weeks later. I am doing 'my thing' and come out to find him in the kitchen with flour everywhere! He had pulled open my baking drawer, pulled the sack of flour out onto the floor, and was sitting in the flour playing and drawing shapes on the floor.

More Art Work – These Kids!

This time I was tending to one of the older children, and had become accustomed to listening for "silence". That was the warning that one of the children was into something truly fun and different. At least for them, it was fun.

I heard nothing from the family room where Shea was supposed to be playing with toys. You know the huge toy box with 50 items he could have chosen. Oh no, he opened the free standing fireplace door. It had not been lit for days, and the black soot was everywhere. That wasn't fun to clean up! He painted his legs, the off-white carpet and the walls. But, his smile was contagious and all I thought about was at least it wasn't the same 'paint' that his sister Erinn had chosen years earlier for her art work!

I do have to say the common denominator for all of my children's mischief was the look of accomplishment and pride on their faces. I had to laugh, that's for sure!

I really look for privacy while I take my enemas. I make noise, it smells, and I function better when I know it is just me, and I don't have to worry about others. When the children were small, and my husband was on business trips, I had to search for time where I could slip into the bathroom or go out to the outhouse. My children don't know how many times I was listening, hopping out just to see what they were up to. Now that I am an empty nester, yes, there is much better scheduling.

The Survivors! Kevin, Erinn, Shea

Erinn, Kevin, Shea, Patty and Greg

Moving Forward In My Life

Running helped me manage my bowels and weight management. This activity helped my overall health by being outside and sweating out toxins. After a good long hour run, I felt light, in tune with my mind and body, and my stomach was flat and less painful. My body became stronger, and I was able to run anywhere, at anytime, and still today enjoy the solitude.

Victoria Marathon

At first, I was able to challenge myself and accomplish little goals. Run to the park and walk back, and then run both ways, each time a bit further or faster. I added distance, speed, and then hills. Every accomplishment gave me confidence that I could handle the rest of the day, and any further curve balls it may throw at me. I also found that when running, I felt more control over my not so healthy body. My confidence became stronger; I was more cheerful and could turn my attention to others' needs before mine. It became a drug.

During the summer school break, I taught fitness to pregnant women and beginner runners. I joined a running group, and the next thing I knew I was a running leader for a marathon clinic. Four marathons and numerous 10k races later, I still run/walk and continue to dance! Thank goodness for the iPod!

A Funny Story

When 38 years old and in for my hysterectomy, I am post operative for 6 days, and am up for a short shuffle, when I come across the ward where I was my first day. I say 'Hi,' to a few of my fellow patients. An older lady, obviously still drugged calls out to me, "Nurse, Nurse, I can't find it!"

I look around and realize because I am wearing a white bathrobe, she thinks I'm a nurse. She is holding tightly onto her bed, and I move very slowly closer to her and ask, "What are you missing? Perhaps I can look for it with you?"

She says, "My thing, you know my thing!"

I shuffle a little closer and ask again what thing was she looking for. She sits up and looks at me. She points to my catheter that is hanging down and she says "That, that's what I'm missing."

I said to her "Well, usually it is attached, so if you don't have it anymore, that must be a good thing!"

She smiles and says, "Oh, thank you, nurse." I reported this to the real nurse, and we had a good chuckle.

1989 Once Again

Only six months later, the pain returned, and I had to once again talk the doctors into checking me out. They again operated and sure enough they had to take out my other ovary and another tumor. This operation was another hell to go through with swollen bowel, etc. This was going to be a hysterectomy.

Menopause/Post Hysterectomy

Not enough is publicly discussed about menopause. For most women, menopause comes later in life. I had such complications with my bowel swelling that the doctors kept me off food as well as any oral medications, such as hormone treatments. Due to this, they put me on a vaginal hormone cream. By the way, this really did not work very well. For me, my doctor suggested I should not go on any more estrogen because I had been on birth control pills for so long. I was miserable. I had the hot flashes, soaked the beds with sweat and my sexual drive changed. In addition to all of that, the vaginal dryness is not fun.

While in bed, my husband also had to deal with a pool of sweat on my lower back if he reached over to hug me. Even my hair would be wet as if I had gone for a run.

I remember one winter I walked outside and sat down in the snow to cool myself off. My usual activity was jumping in the shower and turning on cool water.

I started all of this menopause stuff at only thirty eight years old. At fifty, I asked my GP how long menopause will last. He explained if will just have to burn itself out. I was lucky in comparison to others. I only had these symptoms for about 18 years. Then one day, they were gone and in addition to that, no more periods. Super!

Patty and Greg

After many years of my husband travelling and my high risk operations, we have learned to not take each other for granted. We have valued our time together. We have wanted our children to find a partner like we have. Somehow when the times become more than you think you can bear, remember, if there still is passion, trust, and a sense of humour – don't stop living, keep going and moving forward.

There have been many other surgeries for athletic injuries, removal of tumors and cists, while not life threatening, my attitude was let's just do this and get on with life!

1999 Just Plain Rude

I had been teaching for awhile, and I acquired a reputation as a winning volleyball coach. One year I was taking the senior volleyball team to California for some competition. Policy required that another staff member join me and that we would room together. Although she was an assistant coach in my program, when I explained that she would have to leave the room, or let me have the bathroom every night for several hours, her reaction was "Oooh, you have to do what?" and decided, "I don't want to do that!"

"Nice!" I replied sarcastically. Something or a tone I really hated to use at work. But I was so overworked and exhausted, and I really didn't want to have to deal with her. I had been planning this trip over 10 months. I really didn't want to take this girl, even though I had raised money with my team to cover her costs. Her only job was to show up, chaperone, at times warm the team up while I did line ups for the games. I was very upset and would pay for my own room.

I made an appointment with the principal who was very understanding and embarrassed for my assistant's lack of profession sensitivity. The principal said, "Patty you've never missed work, complained or had this handicap affect your job. Whatever you need, we will pay for it, you don't have to."

Little Flower Academy Senior Volleyball Team, Provincial Champions

2004 Volleyball Tournament

I am coaching at another volleyball tournament, and during a warm up, I made the mistake of laughing. I had leakage, big time! I had to choose which girl to ask to give me her sweat suit to wear. I asked our captain, a taller girl. I'm only 5 feet tall, so I looked and felt unprofessional. Meanwhile, I was not supposed to leave my students, but of course, with bowels leaking that much, I needed to change clothes, and then go lie down.

We did not have assistant coaches in those days, and no parents were attending. I fortunately chose a young lady who eventually became a doctor. Others could see the soiling and so I did not smell sweet. It was lucky these students were older in grade eleven and twelve, empathetic, and capable in helping their coach. I almost cried, but I had a job to do. After this incident, I started to put a kit in the car with extra clothes.

I completed 25 years of teaching Physical Education, coaching track and field, and volleyball. It has been rewarding to see what I taught help these young women improve grow and acquire success. I thrived under the pressure of the many close volleyball games, the strategies and the emotional challenges that came with working with high school female athletes.

2004 Football Banquet

The worst "what to do incidents" was at my youngest son's senior high school football banquet. He was team captain and about to give a speech. I had started a new medication that was to help my bowels eliminate better. Of course, now was the time this medication started to kick in and work. I was sitting in white slacks and all I did was just laugh, and once again I started losing it all.

On top of that I was at a very beautiful hotel, seated at a table with cloth covered seat cushions. If I got up everyone would see my pants and the chair. I just sat there during the speeches. The cramps were excruciating.

As my son was about to give his speech and present his coach with a gift, I leaned over to one of the other parents, luckily a good friend, and informed her of my situation. She said, "Just stay there until everyone is gone."

One of the male teachers came over and said, "Stand up, let me see those cool pants."

The pants had a fun design on the bottoms of the legs. I once again had to think on my feet telling him, "That's ok!" He gave me a hug, and I was very concerned he would get a whiff of me. However, luckily there was not a lot of odor. After his speech, my son came over, and I guess he read my face. He leaned over to ask me what was wrong, and at that time, I started to cry.

He grew up right before my eyes when I really needed him. He sounded calm and gave me his suit jacket. I covered myself up and went to the bathroom and washed my pants in the toilet, yes, the toilet. In his jacket, I had privacy when I took off my pants and underwear. I put them back on and wore his coat and walked straight out to the front of the hotel where he was waiting with the car. Yes, I left without taking care of the chair. I was so embarrassed, although my friend later told me there was not any staining. God was on my side for that one. Yet for the staff of that hotel to this day, I am truly sorry.

This picture is at the 2009 Grey Cup after I had just been bullied in the bathroom. I was fighting back tears, and I am acting! A great big fake smile, but it did make me feel better!. You could tell we were surrounded by the Rider Nation green. While in the washroom stall, I was threatened by two girls who were waiting for me. Of course, the Alouettes won!

Emry Clan following the Alouettes
2010 Grey Cup Victory

Only a year ago, we were in a taxi headed for the airport to fly to Calgary, Alberta, to watch our youngest son Shea play in a CFL football game. I felt nauseous, my stomach was rumbling having taken an early morning enema. However, this time it wasn't my bowels. It was my kidneys and bladder. I had a significant infection, and the antibiotics I was given the week before did absolutely nothing. I couldn't go any further. We turned the taxi around and went straight to the Richmond hospital. The staff put me through more tests, and prescribed the correct antibiotic. Thank goodness, the pain subsided in a few days. Phewwww!

Even now, most of my enemas results are poor, so I am better off taking the enema at 8:00 pm, go to bed for the next 8 to 10 hours, where my system seems to settle. When I start to sleep, I am guessing I have a gallon to four liters of water and waste sloshing around in me. The liquid that does not come out during the enema is absorbed, and then works its way to my kidneys.

The last few years, my feet and hands feel on fire. I get hot and fidget with my feet. It is a daily side effect from taking 5 enemas a day. I try to take them at night, so I can function the next day without the bloating. Even though I occasionally have bad side effects from my bowels, I void all night - about 7 times -, and then wake up with a flatter stomach so I can move. At times, it is extremely difficult to take enemas late at night when I'm tired, so exhausted.

A Good Thing

Recently my family doctor put me on vitamin B12 which seems to reduce some of the problems with swollen feet and hands. He suggested I not eat a lot of red meat which is slow to digest, and of course, he's been right. I feel better, yeah! Gravol type medications sometimes help, so I can sleep, however, seldom do I enjoy a deep restful sleep.

As I write this, I did 'my thing' this morning. I will have to try to not drink or eat for about three hours, so I will be able to wear my clothes more comfortably. It is always a gamble to take one during the day due to the fact I have all that water in my bowel. If I twist, stretch, or laugh I could explode all that stuff out at anytime, anywhere, and ruin my outfit, not to mention my day if I am not at home!

The Blue Bathrobe

When our children were young, I bought my daughter a blue fleece bathrobe for Christmas. She hated it, so I kept it as it is perfect for doing 'my thing', a warm pullover style, and just the right length. It has come to symbolize my daily routine.

What is an enema and how does it work for me?

If you understand the process of an enema, 'My Thing', that I go through multiple times on a daily basis, you will have greater appreciation of how complicated my life has been by including this medical treatment into my routine, family, activities and my profession.

Over the years, my trial and error method had me experiment with different times of the day, amounts of water, when to eat - before or after, and what foods work best in my system, all in search of better results and less pain. I have had to schedule 'my thing' treatment throughout school, university, dating, as a ski racer, raising children, athletic injuries, my career and now the aging process.

At this point in my life I keep trying to duplicate it, a new pullover fleece bathrobe for my nightly date on the can. My husband has also searched the shopping malls for a replacement. Until we find it, the Blue Bathrobe will be an important part of my wardrobe and have a place hanging on the back of the bathroom door.

When my children were still living at home, wearing the Blue Bathrobe was the sign I was busy in the bathroom taking care of my health, or as we like to term it, doing 'my thing'. We didn't use the word enema. It was also a sign to them that I was usually not feeling well.

Add up all of the hours over a year, two hours a day minimum, the total adds up to be a minimum 730 hours a year in the bathroom. Add those hours up over my life, and my point is made. As I think about it, the time spent has been a great use of time, it keeps me alive. As an adult, while doing 'my thing', I like to keep busy reading and learning. I study French, check up on my favorite football team (Go Alouettes!), listen to music, internet searches, emails, work on this book and even watch television in bits and pieces. It helps relax me, and so I don't feel ripped off for my time.

I am away from my husband two hours a night and that is not fair to us; I really love that man! But if it is 8:00 pm, and I start to rustle, my husband automatically says, "Are you going in?"

I am acutely aware of this time apart, since we have already spent so many years away from each other due to his travels for work. I do enjoy the hug I get as I pass him in his chair to go to take *my medicine*, so to speak.

So very bloated and tired, when I come out of our bathroom, I usually crawl into bed to try to sleep.

When my husband comes to bed, we still keep to the pact we made when we got married, a hug every night. And so we do as it always makes me feel amazing. This is another type of medicine.

When I was in my youth, the enema process was shorter, but I must have just sat there, staring at the wall doing nothing. I really wasted years.

So... What is 'My Thing', An Enema?

My Recipe: one blanket, one large plastic bag, one towel, in that order under my hips. I am more comfortable with a small pillow under my left shoulder, and of course, an enema bag and tubing. Add three liters of warm clean water to the enema bag, no mixing required, and a just a touch of good luck, and a sense of humour. Prep Time: 2 minutes. Cooking Time: 2 hours. Serves one so my husband can enjoy a happier me!

I like to fill the container up with water out of the tub, not the sink. The sink tap is usually too small and difficult to fill such a tall container. I make certain I let the water run for awhile before I fill the container. This allows the water to run the pipes for awhile which supposedly gives me safer water. Once I have filled up the water to the top of the bag, I let some of the water out, much like you would if giving someone a shot to get the air bubbles out of the needle. Adding air bubbles to my bowel creates havoc in my tummy.

I lay down on the floor on my left side, tube clamp in my right hand, and I am ready to shake and bake. With my right hand on the clamp, ready to release the water, I slide the end of the tube into my rectum, as high or far into me as comfortable. While on the floor, I balance on my left side and allow the water to flow into my bowel by releasing the tube clamp. To lessen the pain, I clamp the tube on and off in order to manage the flow of water. Once I feel there is sufficient water inside, I clamp the water off, and pull the tube fitting from me.

When on the floor, as I release the water I slowly count to 100, and twist my head around to see what is happening in the container. The entire process is by feel. I put a pillow under my left shoulder and sometimes grab a towel to rest my head on just to help me relax. I wait for awhile, then carefully get up and make my way to the toilet, very uncomfortable, and always in some pain. At times, this means some leakage, 'lovely eh what?'

This is important to know, I do not have a normal anus. I have a ring of scar tissue as I do in my vagina, that at times temporarily blocks the tube fitting going in. The tube fitting can catch when inserted and scratch the scar tissue causing some bleeding.

My bowel has pockets which is called 'diverticulitis'. The water, or slurry can get into the small flesh pockets along with undigested foods and get stuck. Getting up and moving around helps empty these pockets, and a handstand, even at sixty-three years seems to be a good tool. Through trial and error, it seems anything that helps move the water around inside dissolving the solids generates better results, better release and cleansing. At times I find by just squatting over the toilet bowl, my bowel empties easier, but this is extremely messy and never a certainty.

These activities are the sum of the process, and individually only give me partial success, that being a partial clearing of my bowel. When I feel I can release, I have to squeeze my gluteus maximus buttocks muscles tight to keep from losing it while I make my way to the toilet. I usually need to take five enemas a night in order clear my bowel as much as possible. I literally look for clear results in the toilet bowl as an indication of how it's going. As long as what comes out is dark in color, I will keep repeating the enemas, 'My Thing'. Success usually starts to show at the third enema, and I enjoy a sense of relief when anything comes out!

To finish the Blue Bathrobe saga, once I think I am finished or have done the best I can do for the day, I fill the bathtub, and feeling like a pregnant woman, relax and enjoy the lack of pressure on my tummy. If I stand up, the pressure comes back. This is why it is so good to do my enemas at 8:00 pm, then around 10:00 pm I can just crawl into bed, releasing the pressure on my stomach, back and the entire torso.

I get up as many as eight times a night to void the leftover fluid that was hiding in the pockets and absorbed by my body. In the morning I wake up feeling less bloated, and usually tired from interrupted sleep. The last three years I have been losing sleep due to the fluid in my bowel being absorbed and traveling to my extremities. My hands and feet feel hot, painful and usually by the morning I feel closer to normal due to all of the voiding.

Food Glorious Food

I have a love-hate relationship with food. My stomach and bowel hurt immediately after eating, especially pasta, with the exception of smoothies. I love to eat, but my body bloats up quickly. My husband has learned to cook and choose foods that are easier to digest, like fish, cooked veggies, etc. I need to stay away from seeds, nuts and unfortunately pizza.

If I am with friends, travelling, out late, drinking wine I will go to bed and then get up around 2:00 am or later to do 'My Thing'. I find taking enemas during the day causes excess bloating, sometimes nausea, subsequently preventing me from getting any exercise and enjoying life.

Containers – for "My Thing"

Over the years I have had various types of enema containers. They started out as porcelain buckets, thick red hot water bags that got moldy, and now the clear "irrigation" bag and tubing apparatus. It is important to have the correct type of tube clamp in order to manage the flow of water. The enema bag and tubing are not available at every drug store, so I order them from my local pharmacy. I change to a new bag every six months or when it falls apart.

I've had embarrassing times when looking for a new enema bag. Years ago, it seemed I was always trying to explain what I needed to a young male pharmacist and of course with other customers standing waiting their turn and overhearing the conversation. Now the hell with who hears or witnesses the process! This is what I need.

Travel is always a challenge and because of that, stressful. In places where the water is suspect, I try to book ahead to have mega bottles of purified water in the room, or in some instances actually boil the water, and then I let it cool before use. Years ago my Mom got a pill from our doctor to add to the water supposedly to sterilize it. I feel adding chemicals into my system is not the thing to do.

So my dear husband is the best for arranging good hotels when we travel. On occasion we end up with a tiny bathroom floor space. Right away upon entering the room, he will take a look at the bathroom, and has said, "Hey honey, can you take your enema in the bathtub?"

Of course, that would never work, too hard and too cold. One time I had my hand wrapped behind the toilet, my head resting under the bowl, and when I adjusted my body, the tube that is attached to the enema bag came apart. Like a fire hose, the water started to squirt all over the little bathroom. Of course, I react and clunk my head on the bottom of the toilet, then eventually stop the leak. I am happy to be in shape and mobile. Luckily I am able to swear and laugh at the same time. The ironic thing is my swear word at the time is always "shit!" If only I could!

I do believe that every morning we are the architects of our day ahead. We make mistakes, but must learn from them then in our memory box make the necessary changes to not repeat the oversight again. In other words take the good from the error! It takes a sense of humour!

Life is made up of little things, some are road blocks and some are stepping stones, and that has to be enough!

Spilt Milk, Scary And Funny Happened Along The Way

These stories are real: some funny, some sad and some just down-right ridiculous, and all of them occurred during or as a result of doing 'My Thing'. The surgeries and fevers have caused my inside map to be filled with scar tissue. This scar tissue evidentially looks and sometimes even feels like spider webs, and takes up space around my tiny bladder. I am certain that is why my back hurts so much when I am bloated, and need to pee, which is often.

My parents started taking the family to an island on the Sunshine Coast of British Columbia in 1959. At first we rented a cozy cabin and spent eight to ten weeks during the summer school break enjoying the sun, surf and natural beauty of the island.

Wood or fuel oil stoves and kerosene lanterns and candles were the norm in the early days, recently replaced by propane appliances and solar powered accessories. Water was hand pumped from an aquifer that runs in front of the cabins to a tank and then is gravity fed back into the cabins. Still to this day most residents simply use an outhouse, with a deep hole dug to catch the waste and an open 'throne' built over the top. This restroom, was typically located (in back) of their cabin.

At our first summer cabin we were sharing an outhouse with three large families. "What were my parents thinking, with my situation, renting a cabin with a wood stove, a hand pump for water, and no electricity?"

When I asked my father; he really got angry with me, he said "How dare you ask us that, you've learned to handle anything, and we were not going to baby you!"

In retrospect, he was absolutely right, a bit of tough love training served me well over my life.

Our cabin and the settings are beautiful, right on a white sandy ocean beach, with a spectacular view north up the bay. I can sit on the porch or along the shore and hear the eagles, blue heron and gulls. As a youngster; this was the music I would listen to. I could also hear the bugs eating the leaves on a quiet and windless day. But mostly; it was the buzzzzzz of mosquitoes. Around dusk they double in number, and at times seemed to double in size. One year I counted forty six bites on my ankles.

Little Neighbor Visitor

I was ten years old at the time and in the outhouse doing 'my thing'. I hear our little five year old neighbor Lee's voice call from her back door, "Is anyone out there?"

I froze, the door on the outhouse is closed and locked. The only light is what sun streams through the cracks around the door, and it's dark and of course very smelly. I can see out through one larger crack in the door. Lee obviously had to use the outhouse, badly. In her mind 'of course', she lived there; this was her outhouse too. She comes out, peeked in the crack in the door, and saw me lying on the floor with a tube in me.

Lee wouldn't leave and wanted to know what was going on. I really got upset and called out for Mom who rushed out and coaxed Lee away from the door. Things got worse, as the outhouse was near a trail; several families were on their way to the beach with their children who were now curious. My Mom saved the day, but I remember being truly mortified.

Once again, my time was cut short, and I didn't really get to clean out my system, and was not feeling well. The mosquitoes were attacking anyway, and it was time to get the hell out of there. For many years Lee would ask me questions, but much later, I sat her down to let her know what I had to do. I appreciate her concern, and yes, children they are curious. Of course she told some of her little friends on the beach, the rumors started, and I was so very embarrassed.

Slithering Critters

I was maybe ten or eleven years old, and in order to do 'my thing', I had to first boil the water, and then once cooled, fill the red Kool-Aid pitcher container. Out the back door I'd go, and just before I got to the outhouse door, I glance down. The ground started to move at the base of a wall. I see what must be fifty baby snakes along with the mother snake slithering about. I jumped into the outhouse and yelled, "Mommmm, come out here!"

Now you have to understand, I learned my love for snakes from Mom. She approaches, then freaks out and jumps into the outhouse with me!

We are now trapped, and Mom yells to my Dad, "Leo, come out here; there are snakes!"

The snakes were all twisted and coiled into a big moving slithering ball! Dad comes out the back door with his trusty broom, my father's only weapon. As he approaches, the snakes disperse, and he too--- freaks out!

So the enemas in those days in the dark smelly outhouse were taken with a certain amount of fear and trepidation. I had visions of snakes coming through the door while I was on the floor, not just one but in pairs or more. I would skip 'my thing' for days due to my paranoia of the wiggly things.

Truly Creepy Crawler

I was alone at the cabin when I was about 15. We called that batching it. My parents really trusted me. It was a quiet afternoon, so I decided to innocently go about my business. I heard giggling, and thought it was only someone walking along the road next to the sleeping shack. Half way through the process with my stuff there is a loud tap on the back of the outhouse wall. I shook with fright. Bullies can be really creative. Some of the kids that taunted me as a youngster had waited behind our old shed for me to come out to use our open air no door outhouse.

I was paralyzed, and could hear them right next to the outhouse. Having already laid my head down right by the step, I saw it, a large snake slithering right in front of the door. Having been recently painted a bright glistening turquoise, it slowed down and then stopped right in front of my face. I looked into the eyes of the reptile and it looked back at me, both of us, it seemed, were traumatized as the creatures head only slightly moved. I don't know how long I lay there, or how long they waited for me to bolt, but I remember crying quietly, not moving. Finally, after what seemed an eternity, my bullies left. Managing to get up off the floor I of course leaked as I couldn't hold it in any longer. Once I moved to the toilet seat I may have sat there until dark. The snake had stopped moving.

I got dressed, picked up my stuff, realizing I needed to do something with the snake. These kids knew me well. I leaped out of the outhouse, and it didn't move. The snake seemed dead! I gathered up some courage, picked it up by the tail and threw it up into the bushes where it caught on a tree limb. The next morning when I came out I had to fish it out of the fir tree where it was hanging. I still get chills still remembering that one.

I never told my parents about this. I wanted to demonstrate I could take care of myself, and I did not want to give the bullies ammunition to try any more activities along these lines in the future.

Summer Cabin Sunday Mass

I have to go often; pain or discomfort warns me, so I, of course, start to ask relatives and my children, isn't it time to stop. My daughter can go for hours without having to pee. Why can't I? Am I the only one that only lasts for 20 to 30 minutes? Now don't get me wrong, I can go for an hour, even two to three hours if sitting in a car or playing tennis. But I have to be in the right state, you know, not have had any fluids for hours and hours.

Growing up in a Catholic family, we went to Mass on Sunday, special occasions, religious holidays, and while at our remote island summer cabin, we did the trek to the mainland by boat. This meant walking a mile to the boat, or rowing over to the boat, or pushing that big 16 foot boat over the sand flats to get it into the water. It all depended on the ocean tide. Dad would at times get the boat early from the dock, bring it into the shore. If we weren't quick enough meeting him, the boat would go aground. What a sight, an Irish clan pushing the boat off the sand bar, again! We were little kids; Mom and Dad were determined to teach us this discipline. It was usually very stressful! Wouldn't God understand, if we were late?

Other families from the island participated in this trek to attend Mass down in Sechelt. Once off the island and on the mainland, we faced the long and very winding highway drive to attend Sunday Mass. There were times when on the drive down, I would get motion sickness, and seriously need to use a bathroom. Usually, no one stopped, "We're late", and the Mass was one hour long.

I would sit there fighting the nausea, realizing we were going to make the winding 45 minute drive back to the boat, and then the boat ride to the beach. Some of those Sundays, the boat ride was really scary, as the wind had whipped up the waves so it was very rough and bumpy. I never told my parents how sick I felt, although they guessed at times. I think I threw up, at least, half of the trips along that highway.

Once again, I did not like to stand out, and we were taught it is a sin to not attend Mass on Sundays. A few years later, a priest told my parents if it was so many miles and so much work, God would understand. Thank you to that man.

Fishing

Note that I admit I married a man very similar to my fabulous dad. They both love to fish! I will go fishing with them, but only if I can take a book, junk food, and now my iPod so I can dance to the fish gods and plead for the fish to come hither – 'Come little fishies or big salmon.'

Fishing at the summer cabin, I remember venturing out of my warm bed at 6 am to an excited father, knowing we would be catching the tide at its best for hungry salmon. We would pull the dingy down the beach shore edge then row quietly out to our boat. The water was calm, quiet, like glass. A loon would make its morning calls, and I knew I would never forget these special times with my father.

One morning after pushing off from the shore, Dad instructed me to watch his special fishing rod. He was preparing the hook and had it balanced across the stern, and I was not to let it go overboard. We hit a small group of waves and yikes! Over it went, and his look was enough. Oh, the look that only a father can give! But we still went fishing, and caught dinner with the other rods. I know deep in my soul my PaPa loves me. We parents do that.

Salmon fishing success

We had caught the tide perfectly, the fish were biting and Dad was in fishing heaven. I even caught a salmon and was 'happy as a clam'. But all good things have their challenges. I just had to pee and kept asking, "When are we going in?"

"Oh, honey just a little longer, the fishing is fabulous!" he would reply.

Never ever call an Irishman away from his craft. So a little later, "Dad, please!"

"Oh, Mary Anne, just go in the bucket." Or, "Jump overboard, you can swim."

So I did! I just jumped overboard, treaded water and created a safe area, where no fish would dare to venture!

Of course a short time later, my Dad catches a big one, he had fun playing that 36 pound spring. The look on his face was worth my bladder discomfort. This to my Dad is heaven on earth. He said, "I am a blessed man. We are out in sun, being on the calm water, catching fish and hanging out with one of my children!" What a great smile, he had on his Irish face.

Feeding Time

It was such a quiet day, no leaves rustling; you could hear the bugs eating the leaves. It was muggy in the outhouse, and I had just stood up after putting 2 liters of water up into me. I was sweating profusely and wishing I could be in a more comfortable restroom. My normal entertainment was to start swatting the mosquitoes before they got me. I became expert at smashing the side of the wall to kill them. Such satisfaction to see their red bodies smashed on the white wall. Bzzzzz, bzzzzz, 'shit' missed, bzzzzzz, smack – gotcha -Aha moment!

Moving Bushes

As I was just sitting there, I heard munching and chewing sounds. It wasn't the bugs; whatever it was, it got louder and was getting closer. There was the sound of branches cracking under foot. The bushes that were my only privacy started to move. Suddenly, a large male deer, a buck with a full antler rack popped his head through the bushes, chewing his cud.

All I could do was freeze, panic and wonder what I should do. Even though it was a deer, he was still a huge male, and I was trapped. I prayed right there on the spot that he did not feel the same. I did not want him to feel threatened, to attack with his hooves. Luckily I heard my Dad at the back of the cabin. Out of my mouth came a very weak, high pitched, "Daaad!"

He ran out to see what was happening, clapped his hands and scared it away. A few years later there were bear droppings right next to the outhouse, and occasionally on the island there are cougar sightings, so I will take the buck's visit anytime, thank you very much.

Unwanted Visitor

For many years I had no choice but to take enemas in the outhouse, it was our only family bathroom. One day I could just feel there was someone in the bushes watching and waiting. I thought it must be little children playing, at least that is what I told myself. I completed my enema, and as I was walking back to the cabin, wondering how many more times this will happen, I noticed an older boy come out of the bushes, escaping down the back road near where we park our truck. I was too embarrassed to say anything. Once again I did not tell my parents. I did not want them to go after this culprit, as this is a very small and tight community. I felt so very betrayed!

To this day we still have the same outhouse, and yes, we still use it. As a young adult, I started using a Porta Potty and then fifteen years ago, my parents remodeled and added an indoor toilet with septic system. Last summer my husband put up a wall just outside of the entrance of the outhouse to add privacy. Thank you for that, Honey.

I often wonder if any of our neighbors ever questioned what it was like for a small child to spend so much time in an outhouse. While I was in there, I would listen to the kids playing, the hum of the boat engines out on the bay, the jeeps along the dirt road, and people picking blackberries nearby.

The outhouse was about thirty feet from the road. We still to this day have a wonderful wild blackberry patch between the road and the outhouse. Whenever I was doing 'my thing', I would panic at the sound of berry pickers in our patch. They were within twenty feet from outside the lou.

You see, when I take an enema it is noisy, and I never wanted people to know I was in there, or that I was handicapped in anyway. I wanted them to continue to think I was healthy and athletic. It seemed I was always being interrupted, and on alert, always stressed!

Drinking Buddies

Before the house remodel installed indoor facilities, I occasionally would take my enema on the enclosed back porch which only had a bathtub, sink and hand water pump. I had put my Porta Potty in there and proceeded to do 'my thing'. Two people would sometimes visit literally on our back porch steps. I had asked them to respect my privacy which was ignored, or the alcohol fueled their lack of memory.

On this one particular day, I was frozen in my tracks as they literally parked themselves three feet from my little makeshift bathroom door. I was nervous, angry, and not getting anywhere with 'my thing'. To further frustrate the situation, my young children were napping and were soon going to wake up. I decided to wait a bit longer. I laid there frozen, quiet, for sometime, started to cramp and felt bloated. Luckily the babies started crying and asking for me. This prompted these two to vacate our porch steps. Thank God for loud children on that day. My prayers had been answered.

Is Anyone Out There?

To this day, the best way to know if someone is in the outhouse is to yell, "Is anyone out there?"

On this day I was having very little success for quite a while, and Mom must have thought no one was out there. I heard the last two steps as she came around the corner and walked into the door-less outhouse. We were both shocked when she walked in on me. I got so upset I grabbed the enema off the hook we had rigged and threw the whole contraption down the hole. Yep, there I was on a remote island and no other enema bags available. Mom looked at me with disbelief.

I was hot, sticky and frustrated with the whole thing, so I started to cry. I was feeling vulnerable, and I yelled "I never want to do this again; I quit!"

My mother looked at me, forehead wrinkled with concern. She looked like she had done something wrong, yet I knew she has been my biggest supporter since the day I was born. She said, "I am so sorry, and what are you going to do?"

She started to call for my Dad, "Leo come here quickly!" My Dad of course ran out thinking something had happened to one of us. Mother was standing there looking worried as only a mother can.

She started to yell at my dad, "Leo, Patty has thrown her enema bag down the outhouse hole. You have to go down there and get it. What is she going to do?"

My dad just stood there and calmly said, "Martha, I am not going to go into the outhouse hole. Surely there is something else we can do."

I am listening to this conversation and watching the stress level increase. "Leo, you are tall; you can get it!"

Can you imagine? Even if he would have retrieved it, I would not use that enema bag ever again. It would have so many germs; this would truly kill me! Not to mention seeing my poor father climbing down the hole! I just could not fathom that scenario at all.

I finally saw the humour in it all, and started to laugh and laugh. I visually had the picture of my dad rigging up some way to get the precious apparatus back. I yelled "Mom, you have got to be kidding, don't ask Dad to do that!"

They both looked at me and saw I was now laughing. They said, "You were crying a few minutes ago, and now you are laughing?"

I said, "Yes, this is crazy!" After a family discussion, we were all laughing. Thanks to my father, we calmly discussed the healthiest and realistic plan.

I had to go get a new bag. I knew I would have to get into the jeep and drive to Water Bay, then drive my parent's boat to Secret Cove. Then go get the car and drive to Gibson's to the ferry, take the 40 minute ferry ride to Horseshoe Bay and then drive to Steveston where I had more enema bags.

Phew, got it. Yes, this is about a three or four hour trip. I did go back to the city, and all was well. Sorry, Mom and Dad, you're the best, again!

Island Fire-Truly Embarrassed but Hilarious!

One day, I had just returned from the outhouse and was feeling ok. I was looking forward to just going to the beach to relax in the sun. I changed into my one piece bathing suit, and when I stepped out of the cabin, my neighbors were running to a jeep heading past our cabin.

I asked, "What is going on?" And I did not even notice that my husband and daughter were not around.

My neighbor yelled out "fire", and so I just jumped into the jeep, thinking this will be a little fire and I would just help throw some sand and buckets of water on it. I was wrong!

The driver of the jeep kept on driving past the main beach to the boat docks. Greg and Erinn had already gone by boat to fight the fire that was on the other side of the island. I was nervous and to make things worse, I was only wearing my swim suit and my Nike river walker sandals.

Five of us, four neighbors and I, jumped into a 20 foot boat and sped around to the other side of the island. We could see the smoke and flames from quite a distance away. I noticed a forest service helicopter carrying a "Bambi Bucket" already in the air. A fire fighting water bucket I knew well because my husband sold them. I had helped at a few trade shows and knew really only one thing, you don't want to be below these large water buckets when the pilot releases the water. It could crush you.

As we came upon the beach, we saw several firemen and residents, and now I was in quite an anxious state. Where were my husband and daughter?

The captain of our boat started to go into the beach, and I yelled, "You cannot go in there!" This is where the helicopter would drop down to fill the Bambi Bucket.

We decided to go to the next bay. We had all grown up on this island, and were familiar with the bays and trails. It was mid-tide and we knew there were large rocks fairly close to the surface. As we approached the shore, and since I was the one in a bathing suit, I climbed up on the bow to push the boat away from the rocks and to guide the driver to a sandy place on the beach to throw out an anchor.

I saw a large rock and started to lift forward to lower my feet and fend the boat off as the rope cleat -thank heavens- hooked onto the crotch of my suit. The driver backed up quickly so that I could not fall in and be run over. Let's face it, he did not want to hit the rocks either. In an instant I was hanging off the bow cleat, puppet style with my hands and feet dangling freely down towards the clear water, helpless.

Much panic flowed from me, but much laughter from my neighbors and friends. These men started yelling, "I want to unhook Patty!", "No, I will!"

Then the driver yells out, a jokester for certain, "No, I'm the Captain of the boat, it's my duty!"

You could see up my yin and yang, and I was screaming and hoping my suit would just tear and release me into the water. Someone grabbed me from behind, and lifted me back into the boat. I noticed a hole in a most inappropriate spot on my suit, so I immediately wrapped up with a towel.

We helped fight the fire along with everyone else assembled, and then the Forest Service asked us all to leave. The next weekend, the fire marshal came to give a lecture on fire safety, and made sure to mention the part about spandex bathing suits and thongs and how they are not the thing to wear to a fire. Well, noted!

Yes, you have to be able to laugh at yourself. Also I do believe I have had so many men look at my privates, that I was the woman that could handle such an embarrassing experience. Once again, you got it...... It Takes A Sense of Humour!

Hop Scotch - The Search

At our summer cabin, I persevered. I had to try to find a location and system that was close to my babies, provided some privacy where I could relax, and reduce the effort and stress to doing 'my thing'.

Plan #1 -My parents bought me a Porta Potty. Initially, I thought yes, they do listen! The Porta Potty gets so very heavy before I used it, as the top of the unit is for the fresh water, so you can flush. Adding buckets of water, urine and stool made it too heavy for me to lift. I really had logistics problems when I had completed the process, so my husband assisted. However, it did allow me to try using different locations in the house.

Then I tried to move the Porta Potty into the kitchen, but a neighbor came to the back door, luckily, there was a curtain on the window, but I had to be frozen in the tracks again. At least he knocked this time. I did not feel 'pooping' in the kitchen was working out either. Yes, that did not work at all. I felt I was out in the middle of the football field. No, in full view this was just not working for me.

I also tried taking the little Porta Potty up to the second floor, so I could be near my two young baby boys when they were napping. This was too dangerous with just a wooden ladder for access. Moving it after the enema was nearly impossible. As well, I had to clean that sucker inside and out, and it got to be more work than it was worth.

Plan # 2 My family built a new sleeping shack, a bunk house. I tried taking it in there using the Porta Potty. Once again, the children would be sitting nearby on the porch or visiting in the little lane between cabins, or someone would be picking blackberries. It was summer, very hot and to try for some additional privacy, I started not opening the windows for air flow. This didn't work, as the strong smells didn't sit well in a little wooden shack for the next visitor.

Plan #3 Then, at last, about 25 years ago, my parents remodeled the cabin and installed a bathroom, near the new kitchen, with an actual flush toilet. To this day Mom thinks it is *just* for me. That is really sweet of her, and we even argue over this as I can't do that to other family or friends, force everyone to go out to the outhouse with no door.

Patty Peaking Out of the Cabin Lou

Unfortunately, the septic system was not installed properly, as there is no drain field. It only takes a matter of days before the system is backed up, and the toilet won't flush.

My husband and I have had to hand bucket out the one hundred and fifty gallons of waste on several occasions, usually twice a season! Greg now uses the fire pump to empty the liquid junk into the outhouse. Now, that's love. Love that, just love it.

I now hesitate to even go up to the summer cabin when there is a crowd. It is just so very stressful for me to do 'my thing'. The family thinks I can adjust, but they have girlfriends or neighbors come into the cabin at all hours. Then they sit right there in the kitchen to play cards or tile rummy, no more than an un-insulated five inch thick wall away. No privacy for sure, it's very unfortunate. Although my parent's had the best of intentions, it just does not completely work for me. It is the best alternative available, it is certainly cleaner, with fewer mosquitoes and rude neighbors, but still with distractions. I so appreciate the cost, organization and labor Mom and Dad put in to this for all of us.

**How we spend our summer vacation! Some of my loving family,
my daughter Erinn and her husband Colin! Thanks guys!**

Family Road Trips

Also there is my bladder, mostly I just void often. In addition, to my bowels not emptying well after doing 'my thing', I also retain fluid for about eight hours as my body absorbs some of the excess water. Due to the fevers I suffered with as a baby, my bladder has many scars, and I tend to not be able to hold it very long. I can't always keep from involuntarily leaking, especially first thing in the morning.

We were up early in the morning on every road trip. My parents would pack everything in that station wagon, then my brothers, sister and I would somehow find a little space of our own. Although I preferred far back in the station wagon, it seemed I was out of sight, out of mind, and my smaller voice didn't get heard.

My Dad looked so handsome on this road trip to Mt. Baker.

Don't get me wrong; Mom was a genius about keeping us happy. There was always a big picnic basket in between Mom and Dad loaded with a whole turkey, fruit, cheese and crackers and juice. I really didn't have a chance to let my little bladder get empty. I would yell from the back, "Doesn't anyone have to stop to go?" I still to this day look at bushes and passing trees with fond memories of relief. I understand that there are not always places to pull over, especially when we had just pulled over only half an hour earlier, and as the men always say, "We have some place to be."

Skiing

Did you know that back in the late 1950's or early 1960's you could walk, skis still on your feet into a special outhouse, sit sideways, and then get right back on the hill? The building was quite long, and you walked in one end and out the other as too difficult to turn around. It did not last very long as it was quite awkward. I am certain some people really got stuck. I would love to have that back again! Help, where are the women designers when you need them? When skiing and cold, my kidneys would sometimes ache which made me want to 'go' even more often than normal.

Now of course we have to ride numerous chair lifts, traverse across the hills to find a place to go to relieve ourselves, unless we can find a tree or possess a penis. Of course,

I do not have one of those. Even to today I tend to be anxious when I go skiing, and anytime I see an opportunity I will go to the toilet. I would imagine this has been an annoying habit of mine with whomever I ski with, but I get pain in my back if I don't. The problem is I tend to need to go more than others.

Em-Bare-Assed –For Once...Not Me!

I can't go any further without telling this very cute and true story. I was 15, a novice ski instructor, up at Whistler with some friends from Seymour Mountain. We were up the mountain and decide to ski a run called the Toilet Bowl, now part of the Dave Murray downhill.

I started down the run and noticed an exposed bare bum sliding backwards out of the trees, towards the groomed run. This poor lady had apparently hiked into the trees and pulled her pants down to relieve herself. Unfortunately, while in the process, she lost her skis edge and slid back out into the run, totally bare bummed, totally exposed to the elements. The icing on the cake, maybe 'ice' on the cake, she fell backwards downhill, and was laid there screaming in shock and disbelief.

I couldn't believe my eyes and knew my friends were right behind me. I quickly climbed up to her. She was now lying there with her skis pointing up to the sky with everything covered in powder snow and exposed to the heavens. This was not a pretty sight! I quickly took off my skis, my ski school jacket thinking that I could cover her. She was yelling, "Help me get my pants on!"

I was really trying to not laugh. Then the boys began to appear, and all I could do was, yell at them to stop. I released her bindings, helped her untangle, pull up her pants, and put her skis back on. Without a thank you, she skied off down the run. When she was gone, I related the story to my friends, and we laughed ourselves silly. I do recall thinking, 'that could have been anyone', Okay, a female anyone. I felt terrible for her and how badly we laughed. I definitely had a story to relay to my new students about knowing how to set an edge. It was always a good chuckle for them.

Family Perseverance

Our family at Big White: Shea, Greg, Erinn, Kevin and Patty

With these difficult troubles in my DNA, I was quite aware of my children's needs. Of course, I did give them options to go in the bushes, just as we did sometimes while traveling in the car or playing on a golf course. Traditionally for girls, we have been taught to carry TP, as much as we can for the times of need.

Okay, all of those years as a ski instructor did not prepare me for the challenges Greg and I would encountered with our babies and our desire to get them to be great skiers. There were days of fun and exhausting challenges.

The key to starting a family in any sport, especially skiing, is to start them young. While starting a ski program; there are many falls, twisted knees and even tree contacts. It is important to be able to pick up a sometimes crying child repeatedly - many times, put them back on that slippery slope to once again ski. They learned to wiggle their way down the bumps and, of course, as all of the other kids in their age group did, the three of them switched to snowboarding. Such fun! Now when they can, they still go up on the mountain, enjoy the fresh air and live!

Car Travel

Nothing is more special than one on one time with my man. He is a quiet man and a great traveling companion. He never really complains and helps me with everything: my suitcase, golf clubs and always listening to my chatter about, "Look at that cloud, it looks like a matador!" or "Look at the baby colt."

One time I timed him to see how long he could go without saying a word or stopping me. It was three hours. I still now, of course, mention to him my need to stop. As I have learned to travel with tissue paper, I often say to him, "Just find me a tree!" Sometimes he pulls over, but I know he would rather find me a bathroom at a rest stop. We have worked out how to angle the car, so I can hide from approaching cars.

There was the time on our way to the Okanagan just last year when he pulled over at what we thought was a deserted office, and oops! A driver came around the corner and caught me in midstream! Really! At least, I wasn't wearing skis!

Golf Courses

I've had trying times on the golf course, which I am sure men designed. Not enough bathrooms, guys, come on help us women!

There was the time in Scotland at St. Andrews when we were playing the 'New Course' the week following the Open Championship in 1995. I had to pee, so I found an area of secluded Scottish gorse and heather. I started to pee, with my husband on watch duty. Sure enough, a course worker came around the corner. Not fun for me, but I bet I am not the first lady they have caught with her pants down!

Patty at Ballybunion, Ireland in August 2011

I must admit I have to prepare myself emotionally for these possibilities. I do that by telling myself I will play better golf and if some man comes around the corner and gets an eye full he will have something that happened to him, that he will never forget. I will be infamous in his eyes, or thoughts anyway.

My husband now has the habit to point out every bathroom as we pass them along the road, "Do you have to go?", so not to force me to pee in the bushes ever again. See, I have him trained, I guess I am in control.

Cute Little Whiskers

My husband and I were visiting friends in the Laurentians, Quebec, Canada. Their rustic cabin is on a gorgeous spot, overlooking a mountain lake. I typically take my enemas late at night after socializing, so I don't miss out on things. The cabin's quiet, my husband is in a deep sleep when I fill the enema bag full, hang it on the door hinge, lie down and proceed to put the water into my anus. I am lying there quietly, and a mouse enters from under the bathroom door. We both freak out as this cute little thing runs all over, then jumps up and over my hip, and then quickly disappears into the big hole in the wall next to the toilet.

We were staying for several days and nightly I expected his other relatives to pop out at anytime. This does not create a relaxed environment for me. Over the years I've had mice, spiders, lizards, geckos (in Malaysia) and snakes come face to face with me, but this was hilarious.

When Irish Eyes Are Peeping

It was 1978, my husband and I after eight years were taking a long deserved honeymoon vacation in Europe. We, of course, had to visit Ireland. We enjoyed the relaxing rolling landscapes, historic ruins, the pubs and the Irish singing warmed my heart. We especially enjoyed the signs of my family surname "O'Leary" on shops and met some distant relatives. What an experience!

In many older European hotels, they are half floors. It is on these landings between floors that they occasionally put the shared bathroom, normally it's just a closet with a toilet. I carried all of my equipment, opened the closet door and walked up the two or three steps to the small landing. I set up my enema bag, lay down on the floor and noticed the linoleum around the toilet base was looking worn out and even a little moldy. I was careful not to touch this, even though I was in a very small space.

I had to lie down on my left side with my head quite close to the toilet bowl. I heard a noise that sounded like it was right next to my left ear. I assumed it would be a bug or something. After I had completed putting the water into myself, I struggled to get off of the floor. I shifted to my right to gain my balance, looked down to a small hole on the floor only to see an 'eye ball' looking back up at me!

I freaked out then I covered the hole immediately with my towel and sat back on the toilet, emptying myself as fast as I could, then quickly got the hell out of the there!

In hind sight, I should have aimed over that hole – sweet revenge, I tell ya!

My husband looked for the culprit, but with no luck. He may have been able to catch him, if it wasn't for the fact it took me minutes, just to get away from the toilet. I think the pervert was as surprised as I was that I caught him.

Senses On Alert

My husband and I were staying in a bed and breakfast. The hosts seemed like a very nice male gay couple. Their B and B was in a remote forested area in the Okanagan Valley; I noticed the bathroom shower was right in front of a very large floor to ceiling window. The B and B Casita was perched on the edge of a hill, but anyone could stand outside and see into the shower area. While I was preparing my enema, I heard someone or something moving outside by the wall. No breeze that evening, so the wind wasn't rustling through tree branches. I just told myself that these are two gay men, and they wouldn't want to look at me.

The next night we didn't get in until after dark, and one of the fellows seemed to be waiting for us, almost hiding behind a nearby tree in the driveway. How long had he waited behind that tree? Later while doing 'my thing', although out of sight of the open view window, I heard the same sort of noise as the night before. I just felt it was very suspicious and strange, and had a real sense that someone was intruding. We won't stay there ever again!

Even after that experience we had a wonderful time. With our friends, we created great memories in the sun. We did a three hour bike ride, ate amazing food at a winery, and played golf enjoying spectacular Okanogan scenery. At the end of the day we cooled ourselves with a swim and a few glasses of cold wine. Fabulous!

It really does take a sense of humour!

Tired Of The Fight

Attention doctors, interns, family and friends, I am certain there are people who have disabilities, everyday challenges, so that everyone simply thinks they are brave and never complain. They are used to dealing with whatever issues come there way?

Hear this, I for one am sick of being called brave. To me it's not bravery that keeps us going, it's the will to get as much out of life as possible. We have no choice but to move forward.

Doctors moved my bowels around in my most recent operation, and it created pain high up in my chest. In attempts to force vomiting, I tried to stick my fingers down my throat to try to choke and force vomiting, in order to get rid of the constant nausea. I truly thought I was going to die.

Once again I am hospitalized, choking, gagging, vomiting and scared for my life for three days. Finally, I am getting a NG tube inserted, a nasal gastric tube, to pump out my stomach. Once it was in, I could rest.

Personally, occasionally while taking my enema, a dark cloud drifts over me; I don't want to bother. I want to avoid the pain, the bloating and pressure. I wish I could just put something into my abdomen to release the pressure, like letting the air out of a tire or popping a balloon. I really do.

Occasionally when seeing a doctor, they would look at me and say, "You just have a handicap." However, until they hear what I have to say, I don't believe the assumption of "just" should be promoted until the source of concern is identified. At times, even my own doctors barely given me the time of day, "You look so healthy!"

"I feel so crappy!" Okay, I was born with good genes, and I look healthy and am an active adult. Whatever, but now listen to me!

I learned to master the disguise. My plan was to become good at telling little white lies when it came to how I felt on a daily basis. This helped me fly under the radar, when traveling, dorm activity, class rooms, etc. My own children really didn't know what I had to do to live, even when I sometimes ended my day in the hospital.

Rock Bottom

I hit rock bottom today in the fight to pretend! I was travelling for three days; I know sitting for three days is bad. Even the healthy bowel yells out for help with that inactivity. Even though the enema was somewhat successful, I was not myself this morning. I went to my tennis practice in discomfort, pain and back twinges. My inner voice is saying, "I should not be there; I am not able to do this!"

The game was a disaster, and I was in a very foul mood. I just up and left in the middle of the game, walked right out. I needed to get away, and I needed time alone.

If you too, have the daily physical fight, you will know what I mean. I arrived home and tried not giving in to crawling into my bed, assuming the fetal position to cry. I told myself, "What the hell would that do?"

However, I really, really, wanted to do just that, climb into bed and cry. I can't count how many other times in my life I have felt this way. At times I am just tired of the fight, today I hit rock bottom. I try to hide these emotions on a daily basis, but don't want to seem weak or be a burden on anyone. I have been taught I am weak if I cry, or if I quit at something.

I was in a daze, and went for a walk along the dyke on the river where I live. Usually this walk makes me feel alive and invigorated. I certainly didn't want to come into contact with anyone. I had a frown on my face. If someone were to question me, I probably would snap at them. Angry at the world, I was sick of the fight. I was sick of the cheerful and happy act. I was sick of being in pain. I felt like a farce and a failure. My body had once again let me down.

Is this depression? At times I feel a pull, out of control, a Doomsday feeling. I feel I am out of options, and am going to die. Oh God; don't let me go here. I feel helplessness and fear. It is a physical feeling, like a wave that comes and surrounds me. I have always been able to fight it off, but as I get older the more prevalent this sensation is to me. I haven't spoken to the doctor about it because I believe it comes from aging, worries over my health and my daily battle. It does not cause me to cry or lose sleep. It just comes when I least expect it. I only have so much time on this earth, and this is a reflection of my mortality.

As I walked further my inner thoughts were I don't want my friends to see me like this. No one should see me like this. I don't want them to worry, and don't want to have them try to cheer me up. I needed to be with just me. I needed to take care of just me and to think this through. I walked a little further, breathed in the fresh air, and then headed for home.

Sure enough, I see my best friend, she whistles to catch my attention. I thought, "I need to get away." I was caught, she saw me. I just told her in a rather rude tone, "Look, I just need to be alone. I am not good company right now."

Fighting tears, I turned towards my house. She respected my wishes, and we turned away from each other. I actually turned away my best friend. When I got home, there was a tap at my door. Our team captain was standing there. I couldn't just ignore her. I could tell she was worried about me. I opened the door and virtually told her the same thing I told my best friend.

Before I knew it, she was listening to me. We called our other friends. They came over and helped me polish off my birthday present of chocolate covered strawberries. I was coming out of it. I was crying; then laughing. I also realized I have loving friends. Thanks, ladies. You helped me stand. You all rock!

If we are lucky enough to have a sense of humour, let it in. If you are lucky to have loved ones; don't hide feelings from them. Yet- - - that is what I do. I want to appear like I am doing fine as I don't want loved ones to worry.

I lie, I pretend to be fine. Yet white lies and pretending help me cope. It's what I have done all of my life. Besides, who wants to talk about shit, literally spraying all over the toilet, getting on my clothes, and all over the floor? I could not blame you if you were to stop reading this. It is, however, how I feel, and I need to put pen to paper on these issues. Doctors need to know that sometimes we say, "I'm fine". Doctors need to keep asking; don't give up until you get through to us: the writer and reader.

Here is my message. I guess once and awhile, it is ok to hit rock bottom, to have a little, "Why me?" Luckily I have a lot to live for, and let's face it, we only have a one way ticket in this tour of life!

Guilt is good for some things in moderation. This feeling is not a healthy emotion. Banning guilt from my life is something I know has helped set me free. I have been working on this for decades. I am very proud of who I am and how I treat others. I know I only learn from my mistakes and must try to turn those mistakes into opportunity. I recognize the importance of not placing guilt onto others, and hopefully do what is right for them. Life is so very fragile and precious.

Did My Handicap Affect
My Community?

In preparation to tell my story, I sent out a questionnaire to my family, co-workers, and friends. Basically how did my anomalies, my not-so-hidden handicap impact them?

My Older Brother

My older brother, Dr. Dan, was only five years old when he was not permitted to enter the hospitals until he reached the age of twelve years old. He was forced to sit in the car for hours while my parents joined me in the hospital. Growing up, he was unaware how my handicap impacted our lives together.

When we lived in the old house I used my parent's bathroom for the most part, but also started using the kids sal de bain and Dan said he remembers waiting to get in there from time to time. I know my siblings had to miss out on time in the bathroom, especially when we were traveling, sharing one family toilet. He would tease me, punch me on my shoulder, and I just wanted him to stop calling me 'thunder thighs'. So, he was a normal older brother and for children we had a normal relationship.

I don't remember Dan coming to see me at the hospital for most of my surgeries, timing problems. He was a teenager, certainly older, and maybe I was not in good enough health for visitations. I don't remember many other visitors, except a teacher with gifts, the priest, ladies with books to read, the hospital television man, and a friend from work. However, I always had lots of beautiful flowers delivered to my room.

My older brother is a surgeon, his wife is a nurse, and many years ago, suggested I write a book, this book. Recently, he was visiting and had forgotten his suggestion. He questioned whether I even have a handicap?

A few hours later, I drove him to the drycleaners to pick up his pants. I developed serious leakage problems, soiled my clothes and had to return home immediately. He realized I actually do have problems. He was not totally aware of what I go through or what could happen on a daily basis.

I guess he just knew I had physical challenges. I sometimes wonder if he felt neglected when my parents had to deal with my health all of the time. He later told me it seemed normal; it was just what families must do. Yes, that is what our family had to do, and still does.

When I was 19, I needed surgery for the construction of a new vagina and urethra. My brother did come to visit me. He came towards me for a hug and like a wonderful little sister, I threw up all over him. Even though, he was covered with my lovely stomach fluids; he still hugged his little sister, so cute. I was impressed with the love he demonstrated towards me. On this occasion, he brought me Pez candy; I loved those little figures that would open their mouth and spit out a Pez candy. Hmmm, ironic!

Years later, I would visit him and his wife in Colorado. They gave me extreme privacy, and time to do 'my thing' and recover. I reminded them of what I needed, and luckily their home provided it just right. Thanks to them, it was perfect.

Younger Brother

My little brother, Mike, is closest to my age, only two years apart, and as youngsters we spent many hours climbing trees, falling off cliffs, catching frogs and playing music together. In high school, Mike and I were into our own things and did not spend a great deal of time together. I did know he was always in my corner, my little bro!

He is not interested in computers and couldn't respond to my list of questions sent out to the family. I phoned to interview him. I asked him if it was an inconvenience growing up with my physical requirements. Going to school with him, he knew how often I would go home with heavy hemorrhaging and was quietly supportive. Mike had his own serious health problems. At the age of twelve, he was diagnosed with Type One diabetes.

All my immediate family has experienced health challenges in their lives. My oldest brother has high blood pressure, our little sister –Teresa, asthma, Mom a collapsed lung, and Dad has been treated for cancer. Mike's situation was more serious than most. This is why he is so aware of how creative one has to be to navigate through situations with friends, school and health blow-ups. He has to take his pills; he is -Thank God- a transplant survivor.

He was aware of the times I occupied the bathroom as he would dance around waiting for me to finish. Fortunately, my parents had a second bathroom in the house for a family of five. My extended times must have been frustrating for him.

Mike said he was aware I had to fight for what I needed to do. He knew other diabetics, from attending summer camps where he would learn more about his disease and what to expect. He knew I did not have that advantage and had to fight through the ignorance of others. Little white lies go a long way.

He also quietly observed how organized I had to be, to set up my life, to arrange any trips or daily activities around my tough periods and enemas. He learned from my parents about the mechanics of it all. He knew about the mental organization, the worry, and how to cope with doctors who didn't always have the answers. He was surprised I was still alive! Thank you little brother, thank you!

My Baby Sister

Teresa looked up to me. As a little girl around 8 or 9 years of age; she would hang out in the hall waiting for me to come out to play with her. Mom saw this and asked her what she was doing? Mom moved her away knowing it drove me crazy to have anyone nearby when doing "my thing." I really hated the noise – flatulence, I created and needed total privacy. She explained to my little sister what I needed and what the doctors had to do for me.

Then my little sister figured out that if I was in the bathroom daily for, at least, an hour, she could have fun dressing up with my clothes, shoes and accessories. I never knew she did that until we discussed these questions I asked her for this book. Smart business woman even back then, if you see an opportunity, go for it. In hind sight I wish I had the technology we have now and perhaps I could have set her up for some cool photos to put on facebook.

When I had to have the reconstructive vaginal expansion and lengthening, I was really scared. I was engaged to be married and could not have intercourse. What if the surgery didn't work? What if I lost this man? I recall sitting on the steps, crying and yelling "I don't want to go through this again? I am sick of this!"

My dad sat next to me and with a calm voice he would remind me of our faith, that I needed to go through with the surgery, and that my man would not leave me. All the time my little sister was watching. I got up and walked out to the car for the drive to the hospital to prepare for the surgery. She said as she had listened to the conversation, "I was in awe!" Thank goodness for my loving siblings.

In later years, Teresa also noted how she appreciated the way I explained my situation to her children, as we all now share the same outhouse, the one without a door up at the summer cabin.

My baby sister is to this day, probably-with exception of my husband, of course-the closest to me on earth. We laugh together; we love each other's children and husbands. We are best friends as well as sisters. My twin would have been in the mix, too. Wow, cackling hens would be our triangle logo!

My Parents

For me, growing up was very good. My father was well respected and successful in his field. He did so well our mother did not have to work outside of the home. We all lived the good life because of all of his hard work. We were able to enjoy a summer cabin, water and snow ski, and just live a wonderful life.

My siblings and I got along, and even today hang out together. I grew up in a beautiful home in an extremely fabulous part of the city. My mother is my Dad's perfect partner to this day. They have been married for 70 years or so. All of this didn't come easy, they have great faith in God, and tremendous work ethics. They both grew up during the Depression and through World War ll, knowing what it was like to worry about their next meal. They worked hard to build there life together and continue to set an amazing example everyone they touch.

Mom

Mom could not answer all of my questions; it was possibly too much, especially the passing of my twin, and years of caring for me.

Interestingly, in my attempt to fill in the blanks of my early years, in conversation, if I broached a specific incident she would open up and talk about what she went through. Mom spoke of how she had little instruction on how to give an infant an enema and had talked to the local druggist to find out as much as possible

When I was an infant, Mom would give me one enema a day. That seemed to work, but of course, she did have other children to care for, and she administered 'my thing' any time of day or night. Mom never took the time for self pity with what had been happening in her life. She had neighbors across the street with severely handicapped children, and those two mothers became alcoholics. Mom decided not to let that happen to her.

Patty and Mom

Every time any of my bodily functions took over my daily lifestyle, Mom was usually there for me. If she were not, it was because she was dealing with her own health issues. Or, of course we are not in the same city. To this day, if she can't help me with a doctor's appointment, she gets annoyed as if this is still her job. I have a colonoscopy scheduled for this week, not a big thing, and my husband will pick me up. Mom offers every time!

We talked about how difficult it was for her to finally teach me to go it alone. Would I do it right? She worried, would I do it often enough? Would I eat the wrong foods, drink too much, get too bloated. Yes, I certainly did make all of those mistakes.

Mom spoke about the many trips to the hospital in different states and towns. She knew each stop would mean, curious doctors with their own examinations, tests, analyses, and sometimes their own surgeries. She also knew what this meant for me.

She, of course, would worry whether I would meet someone that would love me and stay with me. Similar questions that I wondered about in my teens, would I be able to make love? Would I ever have a family? However, she never spoke with me about these things. Of course, I never really asked her either. I am sure she lost sleep over all of those concerns! She knew I would figure out what to do when off with friends, off to university, meeting the man of my dreams, and figure out a way to have my own family.

Being stoic was what she decided to do, and she would not complain to my dad. She knew my father was worried about paying the bills, working many hours and was travelling to keep our family moving forward. Mom is a positive person. At the times, the doctors would ask her how I was doing and she would explain, "She runs around, pretending to be Elvis, pony tail flipping, and hippity-hopping through her good days."

What more could a mother ask for? Thanks to her excellent parenting, I am still doing that today, just a bit slower and with no ponytail! When I asked her to answer the questions I printed out for her regarding this book, she said, "I should write a book."

I said, "Yes, Mom, you should." Since she does not work on a computer and did not put her pen in hand, I hope this book demonstrates how much input she has had towards the information presented here. I have phoned her many times, asked many questions, each time reminded me how I am so very blessed to have her in my life, and I am proud of her.

When I asked her how my handicap had affected her she would answer, "I am not brave; it is what I had to do." This impacted her entire adult life. She was there for me at birth, as a youngster growing up, and through university. Even through the many recent years of raising my own children, she was there for me. So, for all of that love and dedication, she should get medals, trophies, and most importantly, respect, she has mine!

My mother was also one who could have fun and she is the person who demonstrated acting a little silly when you think you are alone was an enlightening discovery for me. Oh, so that is where I get my little fun times: singing out loud and dancing while doing the laundry or cooking in the kitchen. She to this day has the music blasting in their house and she will still break into her dance moves. I love it!

Once we moved to Canada and I was old enough to understand and notice my mother's good sense of humour. Her way of coping with life was when she demonstrated this personality and great ability to laugh loudly. She created amazing and funny costumes for my father and her up at Buccaneer Bay for the annual summer community sports day. She would spend hours dressing up like a scary mermaid, with black licorice on her teeth and the Lord only knows how she did the tail. Her acting ability and silliness came through when dressed in character. As a mermaid she had Dad carry her to the party across the field. I believe he was the pirate that saved her. They were and still are so very cute.

She also would paint amazing cartoonish things on the walls that made people smile and laugh when they saw the story line behind her mural. She has an amazing eye and sense of creativity.

My Dad

My father has demonstrated interest in this book from the start. He often said how much Mom did for my siblings and for me. But, of course, he did so very much to keep our world moving forward. In the '50's, most women took the role of running the house, and the men, they had to bring home the *'bacon'*. Dad worked hard to bring home the whole pig --- a comfortable life for us all!

When the Doctors told my parents I would need more surgeries down the road, well Dad must have had some panic attacks.

'What am I to do to pay for this?' He traveled extensively, selling as much product as he could to create a good life for the family.

He was doing such a great job that they promoted him numerous times which meant moving his family time and time again. Our journey had the family move from Los Angeles in 1948, to Davenport, Iowa in 1949, to Atlanta, Georgia in 1952, to Chicago, Illinois in 1953, Philadelphia, Pennsylvania in 1954, San Francisco, California in 1955 and finally to Vancouver, British Columbia in 1956. Wow, that is a lot of moving! But, he was always so positive, and when he was in town, always supportive and loving.

My dad refers to me as the "miracle child", and is thankful to God for my recoveries from the numerous life threatening operations I underwent. He found it difficult to be on the road so much, but knew his partner, his wife; could hold down the fort. He understood how difficult it must have been and wondered if I would have a long life. What kind of life would God bring to me?

When I was very young, in grade 7, I started to sprint against the other girls at my school in track. I had just recovered from a recent surgery, and the teachers said I probably wouldn't beat this one girl for a spot on the 4x100 team. Everyone was a little leery of me running at all. Dad being a track athlete in his day was hopeful I would do well, but knew I could have complications. I beat everyone with the fastest time and earned the right to go to the meet and run on the 4x100 team. I did, and I remember even today how very proud Dad was of my accomplishment.

I asked Dad if he was surprised or concerned when I started training for marathons in my early thirties. He said, "No, you had the love of sport, and that it seems to work for you." He knew I was a good athlete from my skiing and tennis successes. So he encouraged me to go for it.

They watched the Vancouver Marathon, and sat along Georgia Street waving and cheering me on, maybe in complete disbelief after having gone through so much with me. I found out later in life that they have always been in awe, amazed that my body with all the daily challenges can also give me so much joy. I had in me, the joy of sport.

My dad nicknamed me Hippity Hop. He enjoys my little dance routines, especially the Irish Jig during our St. Patrick's Day celebrations with 'The Clan'. He'd play and dance with us and still to this day enjoys our company, and we his! He was appreciative of my physical challenges, and how I was able to move well even when so very young. He is still surprised I am alive, after going through so much. He still says, "You're a miracle."

I asked, "Did you ever worry about my relationship with my husband, and how my anomalies will limit our life together?"

His response was that he did think about it, but my husband and I seemed to be in love and living a super life.

When my husband and I put our names in for adoption, my parents were happy for us. They knew we wanted our own clan. They knew we would teach them our faith, the joy of sport and the importance of family.

I asked Dad what he thought about the bullies in my life. Of course, they infuriated him. He knew that I had gone through enough. Twice as an adult and as a professional, I was attacked at work. The first time a co-worker was being verbally berated, and I jumped in, only to have the bully turn on me. Threats, fist in the face, berating jesters and comments.

I asked him how he thought I would handle my life with my husband being away so much. When I mean my life, I mean raising three children. How do you think my children handled me taking enemas? His response was simple, "No different than the rest of your life; we knew you would find a way and fight through any challenges."

I asked my father about any funny stories he might like to add.

"No," he said calmly, "I just remember you had a twin."

I asked about his feelings about her, too. He said, "I often wondered how much would she had been like you?" Always the positive man, "How much more fun it would have been to have two Patty's!"

My father was away for many family emergencies, but he was always there in spirit. When home, he always spent such great quality time: skiing, playing, wrestling, an amazing father. The best! I adore this man and am so blessed to still have this fun loving man in my children's, husband's, now one great-grand child's, and my life.

There is on a few occasions my father had me laughing so hard he got in trouble. At twelve and in for another operation at Vancouver General I was just lying there playing with my Barbie dolls and I noticed a knock on the door but could not see anyone through the small window that is at men's height. Suddenly I saw my father at the upper left corner saying I will come downstairs to see you in a few seconds. What?! Then he bounced from that upper corner and mimicked going down stairs to the lower right side. Then he mimicked going back up and said he had a story to tell me and could he come in. You guessed it I was already giggling and holding my abdominal incision. He had already been noticed by the nursing staff.

He came in and sat down and started reading Huckleberry Finn, but also added a twist of combining Tarzan in the story. His intension was to give me hope to soon be back running, skipping and climbing trees etc. So, he put me in as Tarzan. I was flying through the trees and steeling watermelons and hiding on riverboats. A great adventure for sure! He added crazy voices and had me laughing out loud. He was thrilled I was laughing and by now nurses were coming in the room to listen. I was holding my stomach and yes, I popped two stitches. It was funny to see my father, an executive, to be asked to leave. The story would have to be completed another night.

Another day he also came in to the hospital with Mr. Sanigan a very funny man. They were dressed like two investigators in long coats and of course the business men's hats men wore back in the 60's. They went by the nurse's station and now the nurses were on to my father. The two men did the window thing again and I knew I was in for a treat. This time the two men had a skit they did with many props hidden in the pockets of their coats. With each item Dad tried to not giggle and stay with their skit. They told a little story of where they got the items and what these items could do for me to make me laugh and feel better. To witness this skit was a thrill and this time I had healed enough to not pop stitches and I could laugh out loud. I think I healed twice as fast because of his efforts.

Yes, it takes a sense of humour!

My Colleagues and Friends

In preparation for this book, I asked my colleagues to let me know how they were affected by my hidden handicap.

Their typical reply, "I really am amazed at how you didn't let these handicaps affect your job."

When asked how I felt, I did not want to appear weak, so I would reply, "I am just fine thank you!" Hah, 90% of the time I fooled them all. Of course, I am only human and have at times demonstrated my breaking point.

Ahhh, if they only knew! Wow, I probably should have been an actress. I was already performing a fake role daily. Most of the time, it caused me stress, and I had to confide in some close staff members and friends regarding my hidden handicap. They would cover for me when I would have to leave the gym to throw up outside and until I was able to return to my class. Or, in some cases, when I just had to get home. They would quietly take my class for me. Thanks to those two loving women.

I told one of my administrator's of my situation, requesting access to a bathroom. Originally I was in an office that was right by the bathroom. Then they moved me to a different office. Once again I asked my administrator and her response, "You are not supposed to leave your students." It was not like I left my class constantly, only and just for rare emergencies. These are the reasons my health was kept behind closed doors. It is risky to tell people my situation.

My Children

First of all, I have to say raising three children opened my heart, as a new parent and throughout my life. I became more alive when our little treasures arrived on the scene. To this day, we enjoy every step of their growth and are thrilled at where they are in their lives, especially how they respect and love each other. It is very humbling to see how much they love Greg and me.

Left: Colin and Erinn Aarts, Kevin and Shea Emry, Patty and Greg Emry

These are their responses, sometimes agreeing with one another, sometimes not.

1. Were you aware that something wasn't right or normal with Mom?

The older two children just knew I had to do something for my health and that I needed longer in the bathroom. My youngest said he knew I had to cleanse (a good description) myself, but did not really know what that meant. They all just knew I would get sick if I did not spend the time I did in the bathroom.

2. Besides the blue bathrobe, did you know or were you aware of the time I took in the bathroom? Did you wonder at a young age why I might have been in there so long?

The children all said because they were so young, they paid little attention to how long I was in there. They did say when they were a little older; my husband gave them a little more information. And added, in retrospect, that they hoped they were not too much of a nuisance. Ah, they are adults now!

3. What was your reaction when I sat you down to explain, or did I actually explain it to you?

Our oldest said my husband gave them a little more information when they got older. My middle child said he was not in shock; he just learned a little more of the magnitude. Our youngest was not surprised; he felt it was just the time to learn about more details. And, after travel to Thailand, etc. with the boys, our youngest was glad we had a nice clean hotel – rather than some of the bathrooms we had encountered in public places. He knew the hotel was actually chosen for me.

4. After you read what goes on with me daily, you may think, what's the big deal?

All of the three children were sweet in what they said. They think I am strong. That does help give strength back to me. All three said they have learned the "never quit" spirit from me. They have learned perseverance. I could not be any prouder of that. It is sweet to know they have learned positive things from my handicap. Ahhh, to find positive from negatives is a learned skill, hurray for them! My middle boy added he has learned about being a good husband from this as well. They have observed their father's quiet support.

5. Did you know at birth, only two days old and weighing about 4 pounds, that the doctors cut me in half to partially repair my digestive and elimination system?

They all said I explained some of the surgery when they were little. I actually do not remember that. I guess that is a good thing. That way they just went through their lives dealing with my health issues as best they could. It was their life, too. My youngest said, "I just knew my mom was a beast!"

6. So did you know Dr. Bryans -my specialist in the 60's, 70's, and 80's- told me I will probably not be able to have children, even after he encouraged me to try for about nine years. What a frustrating time for Greg and I. One day I asked the doctor if he thought we should adopt. He told me that I would probably never have my own child.

Then when we got pregnant, my doctor was dumbfounded, along with many people - and very concerned it could kill me. I was healthy, and with my attitude! I thought, 'I will survive this and have a healthy baby to add to our brood of angels, gifts from God!'

My children's comments were amazing here. They all took the positive side. We are blessed with the closeness of the three children. If it wasn't for adoption, Shea may not have had a sister and brother. They are all excited about the new member of our clan -our daughter and her husband's little son. My youngest child said, "How Cool" that it was for him to be carried around for the nine months, and how loving and cozy it must have been.

7. Shea, do you remember the basketball banquet when I had the major accident and my bowel emptied?

Shea's response was he just knew he had to help, anyway he could.

My middle son did not know this had happened, as these situations are very private and extremely embarrassing. Anyway, Kevin was amazed of how wonderful Shea was for me that day. I know my other two would have jumped in to help in the exact same way, the same love for their mom.

8. Have any of you noticed when I have problems, and what were your thoughts? Have you ever discussed it among yourselves or with Dad?

My children did have brief conversations about my health among themselves. They didn't really discuss my enema requirements with their friends unless it would have directly affected them. These were times when we were at our summer cabin or were travelling with families where bathrooms were in short supply. In other situations as a soccer mom, my children had to tell friends bits or pieces when I suddenly was not able to drive the group to a game or practice. Each of them wanted me to know they didn't discuss it with friends. They believed it was simply family business.

9. Did you ever explain my health requirements with friends? Were you worried about their reactions?

Once they are in serious relationships, they have told their significant others. They are all now getting married or are married, so we consider these people new members of the family. Of course, they have the maturity to understand. Also, they are loving towards our family and supportive of us as well.

10.It has been increasingly more difficult the last few years. In fact very difficult as things don't work like they used to. I'm working it out on a daily basis. I know your dad worries about this. Feel free to talk with him about how he is doing with all of this. He gives up more than you can imagine; it is all in the book. Have you thought about what he has to do to help me?

Our daughter has thought her Dad and I have an understanding of how to handle all of the situations. She has said she knows that if we need to; we will let them in the loop. The boys feel their dad is one very important man to us all. They never fully knew the extent of how involved he has been in my situation, but they know that he has been there for me through it all. They all said they see true love and dedication between us through the challenges we face together with our health and other tests of life. They added it is a true testament of what marriage is all about. They are proud of their Dad for being the rock in our family.

11. Have you any other thoughts and concerns? As you can see, I have lots of thoughts. 'Keep fighting the good fight' Mom was their theme. Our daughter says her observations as I have grown older are that dealing with these things is more difficult, and she worries about my future. She wants to make it easier for me.

My middle son says he is proud of me. When I need him, he will be there and that family comes first. He reminds me to keep going and to never give up, and that is what he has learned from me.

Our youngest calls me a beast – a fighter. And, he says keep fighting, the good fight, Mom.

Isn't that great, they have learned good things from me, and I thought I was neglecting them. Thank you, my babies

My In-Laws – They Rock!

Greg, (my other Mom) Phyllis and Greg's brother Scott & wife Helen

Missing is Greg's older brother Les, Scott's wife Helen (His Rock) and of course my very much missed Father-In-Law Rip. They are a positive force in my world.

Early on, a visit to my future-in-laws caused a great deal of stress for me. Please note it was self induced stress. At the time, going in the first time, I didn't know what their bathroom situation would be. Imagine you're trying to make an impression on your future in-laws, only to occupy the can every night for two hours. I worried about what they were thinking at the time.

Once engaged, I still held off telling the Emry family my situation. I had to explain to Phyllis the surgery for the vaginal reconstruction. I can imagine they wondered what this meant for their healthy, athletic son's future. I also had thoughts about this as well.

I remember I needed to tell my future mother-in-law because my future father-in- law made a comment about how long I was in the bathroom. It was not a mean tone; in fact, it was more of a tease. This man was the most loving sweet man on this earth. In hind sight, I probably should have explained my situation to them right at the beginning. As usual I did not want to scare Greg, or them away.

My mother-in-law is so very loving and positive about everything. She is the best mother-in-law on this planet, seriously. I boast about her all of the time. I can go to her about anything, knowing I will not be judged. After many conversations about my struggles, she had no problem sharing her master bathroom with me. We lost Greg's father many years ago, and even now I miss him. My children and I are lucky to have had him in our lives. We miss you PaPa E. Thank you for being in my corner, Mama E. You rock!

Friends

This has affected my very active husband more than I can imagine. Over the years, our close friends have tried to include Greg and I in activities and travel opportunities. Every year there are planned excursions, camping, travel, adventurous outings. Unless I can stay in a hotel away from the activity, fun and camaraderie, we just can't participate. This has cost more than we could afford over the years.

Planning for my enemas makes it difficult to fit me into any schedule, thus adding to my stress. The first thought when an activity is being considered is where and how will I take care of my stuff? My husband and I over the years, have slipped out of our friends radar when it comes to these extra curricular events, and we understand, really! I know that I have dragged my husband with me on this. I wish he would just go and enjoy the activity with them anyway.

Wine tasting in the Okanagan Valley - The Gourmet Gang

I Got Out Of Bed Today!

"I got out of bed this morning", has become my mantra! After spending hours up late with the pain created by the enemas, I had to come up with something. When I retain the fluid, I wake up feeling pretty stiff. To get moving in the mornings, I have to get in a very hot shower, stretch, exercise and sometimes take an extra strength pain reliever. I also ask, "What can I accomplish today?"

Life is too dang short, and so I work on not wasting my days. If I'm not feeling well, I do spend some extra time in bed. This lack of something to do, 'for me' is rare.

Giddy UP!

As a teacher before I would dismiss the class, I would always ask them, "Now, girls, what did you learn today?"

They, over time, knew I would ask, and these young minds would actually remember and respond with the 15 to 16 things I had set as the goal for that lesson. What was really rewarding' was it made them think, listen and appreciate what they learned. At least, that is what I have told myself after all these years.

I challenged myself to make it interesting and fun. I had to sell my product. It was my job to sell every day the power of knowledge when concerns to personal health and fitness. It was my goal in life to teach everyone and anyone I met the power we all have to choose one's own healthy lifestyle.

My theatrical side as 'Helga the Ski Instructor'

I like to ask myself at the end of the day, "Were you able to overcome or did you give in?", "Did you get out and influence others to persevere?", "Did you learn anything about yourself" and, "Mary Anne did you check in on family?"

These lifelong habits have helped me think more clearly and deeply, speak more positively and have mannerisms that will demonstrate my confidence and happiness. I don't spend too much time wondering how I will take enemas, and do plan when. I pray to be blessed to live an active life with my wits about me . I believe staying strong physically and mentally will aid in my daily medical requirements.

As an aging athlete, I have now developed arthritis, patella tendinitis, meniscus tears and chipped bones in my knee at the bottom of my right femur. I am now waiting for surgery for my knee and hip. Here we go again. Whatever, I will deal with that! I tore up my knees and shoulders from skiing, tennis and volleyball. I jumped, leaped and had fun when my body would let me. Now I have to make some difficult decisions, is it time to quit skiing, tennis, running and golf? Unfortunately, I hear yes, more than, "Hell no girl, get your butt out there and live!"

The way I have lived my life, has always been to "Just Jump In and Do It!" Passion goes a long ways.

When I am no longer able to play tennis, I have hobbies, I hand paint wine glasses, pottery and dishes. Fortunately, I love my hobbies, socializing and making people laugh. These are some of the things that fuel me to keep going. If you ask me, "How are you this morning?"

Even if I lie, I feel better because it is a positive response. Sometimes when it is someone I am close to, I will say a couple of sentences to let them know where my health really is. Okay, let's face it, actually everyone, even doctor's eyes glaze over if you tell them too much negative information.

2012 Steveston Community Ladies Tennis Team

My father and I were talking about the book he is writing on life and business career. The similarities are amazing, demonstrating how strong we have had to be. If others can learn from just meeting us for a few minutes a day or becoming friends, and we can influence them, brilliant! Yes, we did something good today, we helped someone out.

I've discussed with family about the times when teaching a class and my bowels emptied, forcing a quick scurry from a very busy cafeteria, down steps, to the washroom, wash my clothes, change without being seen, and get back to my energetic Grade 8 classes. I hid so very much, I was a master of excuses when this happened. I had a family, a mortgage, a husband that traveled; and I had to keep my job. I would lie daily about how I felt.

Strut - Coping Tools!
The Teacher In Me!

Cognitive Silence

Cognitive silence is something I have practiced for years. It comes in different forms: remember when the kids are screaming, or the noise at work is so loud and if cognitive silence – zone is practiced enough; you can get yourself into that state. People do relax while on the toilet, and sometimes they are not aware of the fact they are going into this silent place.

Differential Relaxation

Fortunately I have practiced *"Differential Relaxation"* and have introduced it to my clients. I learned about this form of stretching and flexing of muscle, breathing skills and relaxation years ago when I danced for "Orchesis" at university. My experience with this has helped me tremendously. This practice is similar with Yoga. I love the practice of listening to one's own breath. Getting in tune with your breathing is a great tool, especially if you are in pain, or physically and emotionally uncomfortable.

When there is an apparent situation with stress, whether physical or mental, I have used this technique. It keeps me from going crazy, hitting things, from giving up. You know the times when you're waiting in the doctor's office or at home by the phone for the news: Will I have more surgery? Is this one going to be the C word, cancer?

Differential Relaxation Practice

In a warm room, lie down on the floor on something comfortable. Stretch your arms and legs out long and arms wide. Feel the ground beneath you. Try to melt into the ground. Cognitively scan your whole body; feel all of the spots? Proceed to breathe in, then take another large breath, and blow it all out through your mouth until your lungs are empty, and you to the point where you feel you may give out a little cough. Rest and listen to the silence. Listen; really listen to your breathing. Is it slowing down? Repeat the breathing procedure once again. Listen, listen and listen some more. Now, tighten you right foot, and try to relax every other muscle in your body, then slowly release the foot. Listen, breath and listen some more. Alternate parts of the body flexing and relaxing, flexing and relaxing. It will take awhile but you can go through the entire body, flexing a muscle, then relaxing that muscle, and remember the facial muscles, your core. Take in the sound of Silence, Breath and just be!. Enjoy that silence.

Deal with it!

If we are waiting for results from one of those big life decisions: a job, health results or relationship issues, then we need to face these challenges head on, and take the steps to move forward. Distraction is a good management skill for stress, and talking about the issue, setting and initiating a proactive plan is empowering.

Silence, Nothing, Rest are All Good

I never taught my children this skill, but I did teach my students. They would fall asleep, walk slowly out of the gym wrapped in a blanket I allowed them to bring to class. They told me time and time again how refreshed they felt. There are studies that prove we are all sleep deprived, and if we take time to rest during the day, even five minutes in a quiet place will create a more productive day.

One of the elements of physical fitness is rest. I taught my students to rest. I loved it, as on occasion I would have to wake up a few 'sleeping beauties' to get them to their next class.

At my age, I have more opportunities for rest, and I admit I love taking a nap. In order to get to the state of 'nothingness' where we block out noise, movement, worry, the to do list, think of nothing at all, just drift to another zone. Think of something or do something that is boring, or repeat a word over and over....

The mental training of this is used in other activities, and forms. In example, while running marathons it is common to put one's self into a mental state, 'in the zone' of "one foot in front of the other" again, again and again. They are far beyond the 'my knees or back hurt', they just repeat the same simple running and breathing exercise. I apply this to my running from time to time, and daily I use it when I am doing 'my thing', or just when I am trying to get that nap!

I choose not to go to that place of pain, depression, and fear. I select a tool from my arsenal to use for help. In other words I have to make cognitive decisions to distract myself by the use of my music therapy, or playing solitaire, even doing light chores, laundry, or watching a comedy on my computer. Breathing exercises are always beneficial to coping with stress.

I studied yoga while at university, and then again in my teaching career in order to introduce the discipline to my students. It was amazing how my students and I would get into positions, hold them and not break. My favorite, 'downward dog' felt really good for my stomach. And, once again, the instructor would remind us of the importance of breathing during the exercise. Some of the moves are difficult I would catch myself holding my breath, and again the reminder to breath. Very good!

Focus on Pain

Another tool I promote really takes practice, but it has benefits. Mentally accept the pain before it happens, acknowledge it's coming, and understand what it feels like before it occurs. Accept it and breathe again. Certainly, if you have felt the pain before it is easier to accept it before it occurs the next time.

If you are going through a treatment, ask the doctor, dentist or nurse for a break once and a while. This is a good way to let them know your pain tolerance.

A comparison to consider is you know what really cold water feels like? Suppose someone is going to throw you into ice cold water. Most of us can remember the shock of ice cold water, the sinking into the cold, water rushing up our spine, encompassing our head, etc. The cognitive thought of this is 'I know what this (experience) feels like, and I can manage it, breathe, and cope.' In fact you may not react much at all. I call it, "*pain recognition, and repetition*". In other words I can plan my reaction to generate some self control.

Patients who have daily or weekly routine treatments create an *acceptance*. I personally have no choice, and have found the more I fight, the more discomfort I have. I know what it feels like, I have survived this treatment daily, and I know what the side effects will be, breathe and get through it.

Visualization

Is a powerful tool, and I am a visual learner. I mentioned before about my special place. Numerous thoughts go through my brain when technicians are taking more blood, or inserting a catheter, root canal, etc. I simply focus on my children's faces, the mountains, the Fraser River, eagles souring in the wind…..happy things and places! We all have them, and are blessed when we can call on them to help us through a trying time. The key is to mentally recall that special place in uncontrollable situations that create stress in life. Think of memories that will make you giggle out loud. Like this following picture.

This is our grandson "Emry" on his first birthday. When I remember this photo I can distract myself from pain. It makes me giggle out loud every time. He was so proud of himself, and I guess I didn't give him enough space. Luckily, I love chocolate!

I have added this amazing photo to point out my retreat. I am standing on the beach that has over the years been my focal point when I mentally needed to be in a positive, happy place. Now as an adult, yes, I have a glass of wine in my hand, and it's at sunset. I focus on the times when I'm walking along the beach with the warm sun in my face, wading in and out of the tidal waters, breathing it all in! It's a beautiful long remote beach with resident Bald Eagles, huge clay cliffs, white sand beach, harbor seals playing off shore, and the incredible the view of the inside passage and Vancouver Island in the distance.

A few years ago, I discovered that one of my sons also uses this exact same place for his solace as well.

Other Distractions and Places of Solace

Sports have been great for my physical and emotional strength and health. The ego is a wonderful thing. How many of us have hurt ourselves? We are in pain, but we tell our team mates, "I'll be fine!" When in reality you're not. This is another cognitive decision we make to manage our pain. Injured, we will *breathe* differently, more rapidly, and experienced coaches or trainers will encourage slower breathing to calm the body.

Hard exercise like my running, or loud music, boxing, hobbies are also distractions that can be successfully used to get through difficult times or pain. When I paint I do find myself thinking simple, flowing, artistic nothing thoughts. I am in my own universe, not aware of anything outside my paint brush and my art.

The key is to find more than one coping skill. It is healthier to have more than one thing to rely on. Hobbies, *music*, reading, work, etc., can keep us thinking and busy.

Audit your body

All of us, even the handicapped, when we realize a success in life, or a simple achievement will display our emotions, and that positive empowerment of the moment. We open up our body, stretch out our arms, become as big as possible, occupy the space, it creates a positive confidence. This is something I do frequently, especially while running, it just helps get me fluff my wings, puff up my chest, and creates…awesome! This can be accomplished sitting, standing, or just taking up space. A smile will take control of a room!

The opposite is true. If we collapse our body this can change our mind to negatives, creating weakness or a lack of inner strength or will power. So try to take more risk, think abstractly, be assertive, optimistic and see how that feels. Women are not as good at this, but we can still assume those confident stances and gestures. If you need a tool to smile, place a pencil horizontally in your mouth and watch that little grin appear! Whatever works, right?

Prayer

Is our miracle conversation with God, maybe more listening, than wishful thought, talking or pleading. I have used prayer my entire life, and daily. Even when the outcome of my operation was potentially life or death, and totally out of my control, thoughtful prayer prepare me to mentally handle the pending result. Thank heaven, I have a faith which is supported and shared by my family. As I entered surgery, I had no other choice but to place my life in God's hands. Just breathe deeply…and I was calm.

Reward

It has been fun to reward myself over the years after conquering obstacles. No matter how small my gift to myself was, it helped to reward overcoming the challenge. In fact, this is a big thing. Add up all of the little rewards, and you can fill up your confidence bucket.

Time

A must for healing is *time*, we need to give ourselves *time*. I always need to know a timeline. It helps me plan, and prepare for what was happening. I constantly asked my doctors for a timeline, "How long will this take? And, When will I get out?" Once I had a general idea of my future time line, then I would just go through it, mentally prepare, take the time and adjust my life.

Strut

Here is one I use to pick me up. It may be weird but it feels great. *Strut* yes, strut. I told my students, "Strut to the base line before you serve the volleyball." Take command of your situation, be proud, like the world, own yourself, and bet on me, I Rock!

Even when you are anticipating scary news, if you can muster just half a strut it will help brighten the day. In other words, attack it head on, brings it on!

My best friend knows what I mean. Once we were in a tennis match, and she was having an off day on the court. I told her to "Strut!" "Stick your chest out and show you're a confident and powerful woman!" It worked! Of course it doesn't hurt to do the preparation or practice knowing you're prepared and have the tools to back up your confidence.

Color

Another trick I really like to employ, *color*, in my case bright lipstick. Color looks back at me every time I apply it in the mirror. I put it on for me. Yes, wear hues, think rainbows, dress up your food and decorate with color. Living in Canada, we don't always have bright blue sky, so buy fresh colorful flowers and adorn your home!

Family and Friends

It is my goal to surround myself with positive supportive friends. There is no place in my life for a bully! *Reach out to ask for help*, and make it clear that you need them. Don't always try to be brave. We tend to protect our loved ones from the worry and pain that they feel for our struggles. At times it is healthy to let them see we are all vulnerable. Enough of the false bravery, otherwise, they can't tell what is going on in our head, heart and life.

I have found the more I have opened up about my handicap, the more I find out who my true friends are. The best of friends are the ones that not only put up with me, but will also hold me accountable. These are the people who will help drive you to doctors, take care of your kids or your pet when you need them. Remember to thank them, and be supportive for them as well, pay it forward! Love them back and take the love as once again it is like a smile it is free and wonderful.

Smile

I love to *smile* at people, and I always will get one back. It works, it's a quick fix, and it's free! Here is a free one, Look in the mirror, smile, even laugh out loud, Yes…Laugh Out Loud!

Give Strength to Give Back

I do like to ask about my friends and family. People love to be asked about their latest drama or accomplishments. Take time to listen, show you're a friend, demonstrate your love and empathy as for some to share deeply it takes time. This really does make me feel better to think of others and what they are dealing with first. I will say positive things to them and tell them a reason why I love them. Often, they will give back positive stuff too!. Then, it makes both of us feel awesome! When we get involved with others lives or concerns, it is extremely rewarding.

What is my potential?

I ask myself what is my potential? I have lots of potential to learn, live and move forward with my dreams and goals. I keep a record of all the good things I have done in my life. Learning the value of hope and faith was important to live my life positively, and I still have a lot of living to do. Knowing my potential to be brave and courageous helps me meet challenges head on.

The bar is set, and my expectations are high. If I'm not satisfied with some areas of my life, I always have an open opportunity to reset realistic goals.

I want vs I need

I try to listen to what I want in life and make short and long term plans to achieve these targets. I try to stay away from what I need – it is a negative thought practice and can get in the way of achieving what I want. I want should be clearly defined in your thoughts. I want to just be me – a strong, cheerful survivor. Once we let go of, 'I need' we are no longer going to act and be a needy weak person. This drives feeling good and reduces procrastination of moving forward.

Know your worth

We all need a sense of worthiness. What are my talents, skills and who loves or likes me? Am I good at what I do? Only you know this for certain. If you don't feel needed many of us have a hard time, and may ask ourselves, "Why am I here?" If you know you can keep a job, take care of your physical being and keep out of trouble, you are creating a sense of self-worth. There are so many other elements in our lives where we earn or generate self worth. If we are great just being by ourselves we have taken the first steps to being productive and worthy.

Through our actions we must demand respect, because we have earned it. Every human being has value. Create a plan of short and long term goals and objectives, the commit to following it in order to move forward.

In a Nut Shell

+ self edit

+ faith

+ color

+ healing time

+ breath

+ hobbies

+ spend time with positive friends

+ smile at strangers

+ Sport

+ give away strength

+ nothingness

+ silence

+ strut

+ rewards

+ friends and family

+ yoga or something like differential relaxation

- focus on the actual pain

- Visualization skills and, you can probably add more.

- What is my potential

- The Bar I Set

- I Want vs I Need

- Know Your Worth

I have got to leave you now, I am going to smile to some of my friends, think and speak positively and ask them about their day.

Balance Forward –
Life Style Coach

Overtime following my teaching career, I developed a desire to build a business teaching health, fitness, and wellness. Helping people to develop a contagious positive control in their life.

During my teaching career, I collected information and started formatting my mantra and how I would pursue retirement and a new business. I started planning retirement. A direction makes it much easier to make that jump.

Along with meeting with my financial advisor at work, many discussions with my husband I still was not ready to retire but felt better about what I would do to fill my time.

I now enjoy helping women take control of their life and future wellness. To finally challenge their willpower, eating habits, time management, goal setting and to understand fully what their safe healthy choices are. I specialize in helping middle aged women, much like myself, to face their challenges head on and use a positive assortment of tools for their recovery, and future wellbeing.

There are many tools on my website **www.bfjumpin.ca.** Enjoy!

The following are a few references:

> "I'm very pleased with the lifestyle and fitness coaching that I've been receiving with Patty Emry. It's easy enough to set goals, but another to set realistic goals and then to act on them and to continue with the lifestyle changes needed to meet these goals. Patty has helped me with my planning and goal setting, giving me the tools to do just that. With her guidance, I've set goals that meet my needs and my fitness level. I value her commitment to me and helping me to succeed. I now know that I can have a healthy relationship with food and am working on food being a fuel source, instead of a reaction to stress and/or boredom. She's very knowledgeable and encouraging while sharing her

expertise in a fun and safe environment. In addition, her positive energy and attitude are very motivational which is really what I need. It feels great taking the right steps, and having the support while on my journey to a healthier me!

You're awesome Patty, thank you!!!"

Ramona

—

I started with Patti about four years ago.

I needed a life coach. I have had other fitness trainers in the past, and they were fine. Life happened, college passed, I got a desk job, and suddenly, life was no longer healthy and the body suffered. Patty offers just what I need. And I was ready. I really needed a teacher. I needed to learn to integrate healthy life choices in my everyday life. Patty tailored her program to meet my needs and abilities. She provided tons of practical tips and ideas to build a healthy and balanced life.

The most important part

of all, when working with Patty, is I feel safe. I trust her. She knows here stuff and I can sense she is truly experienced and confident.

She absolutely loves helping people live better lives. Maybe Patty's coaching is just what you need to balance forward."

Suzanne

—

"To anyone who might be looking for some life coaching, Patty Emry is really good at it. Her back ground is well suited to get you in shape in a safe and enjoyable manner. She will prompt you to do your very best and be there for you to answer questions and get you going. Patty is always a pleasure to be around even when the workout is grueling. I would recommend her to anyone who was looking for a life coach."

Karen McDonald

It has been a joy and rewarding to test my knowledge learned over a career as a teacher, and learned from my own hidden handicap over 63 years. It's truly a pleasure to work with so many wonderful motivated women, whose objective is to absorb and learn as much as possible from my experiences and knowledge to positively impact their future lives.

My message for all is to remember that we can still make positive change in our lives, there is no end to positive opportunities.

A Patty mantra has always been that my hidden handicap does not define me. I have accomplished much in my life. No matter what, dance through life and wake up giggling!

Surgical And Exploratory Operations / Family Moves Time Line*

The last part of this memoir is my life timeline and then the surgeries and tests. Please take the time to read them, be prepared for whatever it leaves you with. It looks worse when you see so many, but I am now in my 60's and have a super life!

1948   Parents and older brother move to Davenport, Iowa, U.S.A.

1950   Birth November 2, 1950, in Bettendorf, Iowa, U.S.A.

1950   Major life saving surgery at two days old, created exits for GI, reconstructed stump and pulled bowels into place.

1951   My twin sister passes away January 25, 1951.

             Family moves to Atlanta, Georgia, U.S.A.

1952   Family moves to Des Plains, Chicago, Illinois, U.S.A. Dr. Potts – Children's Hospital

1953   Family moves to Media, Pennsylvania, U.S.A. Urethra, kidney and bladder surgeries and series of visits to treat infections and fevers.

1954   Kidneys infected, Moturia treated by long term chemotherapy – Chicago corrective surgery to remove flap over urethra. Family moves to Los Altos, California

1956   Family moves to Vancouver, British Columbia, Canada

1958   Serious Alergy bee stings

1962   Surgery required for the imperforate vagina to allow evacuation of menstrual flow.

179

1963	Fluid cyst found and taken out, a second mass identified as potentially cancerous.
1965	Age 15 Teaching skiing at Mount Seymour. flipped in the air and landed on my head suffering a concussion, headaches and vomiting for days.
1966	Age 16 Skiing down the cut at Grouse Mountain; I flipped up in the air and landed on my left shoulder, dislocating it. The doctors wanted to put in a pin, but that would mean more surgery. They said I might not need an operation if I kept my shoulder stabilized. So I avoided that operation. Taking enemas with that was really tricky--- as I use my arms a great deal.
1967	Vaginal blood flow restriction with infection; underwent a procedure to drain system.
1968	Skiing injury, on crutches for a month making my balance and enemas very difficult.
1969	Dr. Ankerman identified urethritis and bowel knuckle type tortion requiring additional surgery. Upon examination a knuckle in the bowel was discovered resulting in surgery during my senior year exams.
1970	While attending University I suffered from chills, nausea, fevers, and more infections (pyelonephritis) urethritis requiring antibiotics.
1970	Surgery to urethrotomy to open Urethra, and vaginal track, Dr. Longpre.
1971	Married August 28, 1971, Prescription for premarin estrogen containing (birth control pills.) Skiing injury again! Crutches for over a month.
1972	Onset of headaches – I thought it was from stress induced. I had much vomiting, dizziness, motion sickness, vertigo, and sharp pain in right eye.
1973	My husband and I move to Vancouver, finish my university degree. I had severe migraines.
1974	New teaching job, elementary school Physical Education, coaching and school secretary. Back issues, I was diagnosed with severe scoliosis and kyphosis. I was warned I should not teach physical education or coach for risk of paralysis.
1976	I experienced continuing migraines and toxemia.
1981	Adopted first child – beautiful little girl, Erinn.
1982	Migraines, vomiting – finally went off premarin birth control pill. Headaches went away.
1984	Adopted second child – handsome little boy, Kevin.

1986	Gave birth to our youngest son, Shea Christopher by caesarean section,
1988	Anesthetic vaginal investigation found a mass on the left ovary, and another near the right ovary, hysterectomy surgeries to remove both masses.
1989	Bloating– saw Dr. Ankerman - bowel problems
1990	Back problems
1991	Tumor under right shoulder removed
1992	Two vaginas notes and tests completed
1993	Lump in left breast tested and resulted in a lumpectomy.
1994	Nodule found on my vocal cord.
1995	Right hip surgery to remove a fatty tumor, and examination to check for skin cancer on back of left knee, benign.
1998	Severed left Achilles, surgically repaired, off work for four months..
1999	Heart palpitations – halter monitor arranged.
2001	GI Problems – Vancouver General Hospital –Dr. Anderson
	Volleyball accident, severed an Achilles tendon, off work four months. This was a challenge.
2003	Bowel Examination – Dr. Fishman
2004	Cyst on right hip removed, tennis ball in size.
2005	Voice tests – Dr. Wong – losing voice at work.
2006	Pneumonia – missed three weeks of work
2007	St. Paul's Hospital examinations for heart palpitations, tests completed without solution. Extreme pain both knees – Dr. Taunton – needed to lose weight and strengthen quads. I had patella femoral syndrome – strengthening exercise and weight loss recommended.
2009	Small tumor removed from hip, off work one week. I retired from teaching.
2012	Maintaining regular enemas – not great. But, this is better than the alternative. - Every two years colonoscopy –This preparation process was brutal preparation for my colonoscopy – house and bed bound enemas.

Medical Reports

NOTE the Doctor's medical reports and letters of my early examinations and my surgeries are reprinted and inserted respectively.

Surgeries Reports from 1989 to Present

Note* I was going to do some drawings to simplify the vision of these surgeries, but decided to just leave that. It would probably look somewhat like spider webbing at this point.

Hysterectomy

April 25, 1989 VGH Dr. C.W. Carpenter, Dr. D. Millar Left Pelvic Mass/left hydrohematosalpinx, bicornuate uterus with double cervix and duplex vagina/laparotomy with total abdominal hysterectomy and left salpingo-oophorectomy.

Procedure and Findings: Under general anesthetic, the patient was initially prepped and draped in lithotomy position and Dr. J. Ankenman carried out a cystoscopy and placed ureteral stents bilaterally.

The patient was then reprepped and draped in the supine position with two urethral stents in place and a Foley catheter in place.

The abdomen was entered through the previous lower transverse scar and the subcutaneous tissues were sharply dissected down to the fascia. There was a dense amount of scarring in the subcutaneous layer, the fascia was then separated in the midline and dissected superiorly and inferiorly up of the underlying rectus muscles. This was carried out using sharp cutting cautery because of dense adhesions. The peritoneal cavity was then entered in the midline without difficulty and the bladder was stuck high to the abdominal peritoneum, and a window was carefully dissected down around the bladder. Some bleeding points were tied on the dome of the bladder.

The peritoneal cavity was now opened without difficulty and initially saline washings were taken from the pelvis. Following this an examination was carried out which was somewhat limited because of the adhesions and scar formation on the right side from a previous laparotomy. However the liver surface appeared normal as did both kidneys and the upper abdomen felt normal. I could not clearly outline the gallbladder because of adhesions in the pelvis. The aorta and pelvic vessels all felt normal. The uterus was completely bicornuate and the right ovary and tube were normal except for a 1 ½ cm physiologic cyst on the right ovary which was left in situ. The left ovary was buried underneath a large distended tube which had the appearance of a hematosalpinx.

As well there was another separate hemorrhagic cyst on the top of this tube which was not clearly endometriosis but appeared to be another collection of blood in the peritoneum overlying the tube.

The bowel was then packed back out of the abdomen and initially a self-retaining retractor placed in the wound. Initially the sigmoid colon was cleared from the left tube and the peritoneal side-wall was opened without difficulty. The infundibulopelvic vessels were clearly identified and clamped and sutured doubly with #1-0 chromic catgut suture. Following this, the cyst and ovary were sharply dissected away from the side-wall peritoneum and throughout this dissection; the ureter was clearly identified with the aid of a stent.

At this point the anterior pelvic peritoneum was dissected down around the lower segment of the uterus. However there was much difficulty in the midline because of scarring related to the previous Caesarean section. The left round ligament was identified, sutured and separated during this dissection.

On the right side, the right round ligament was clamped and tied and separated and the anterior pelvic peritoneum identified and dissected to meet the left side in the midline. Following this the ovarian pedicle was clamped across using a Roger's forceps, incised, sutured and tied, times one using #0 chromic catgut suture, thus preserving the right ovary and tube. At this point further dissection was attempted on the bladder, however it was very stuck up high on the lower segment of the uterus and this was removed with sharp dissection using a scalpel and actually removing some of the myometrial fibers along with the bladder.

The uterine arteries were then clamped on either side and sutured with #0 chromic catgut suture. Following these parametrial tissues were taken very carefully and incised, sutured and tied with #0 chromic catgut suture. At this point it was clear that there was still a good bulk of cervix and the bladder was very difficult to dissected very much further so the posterior pelvic peritoneum was entered and sharply dissected away and following this, both utero-sacral ligaments were clamped on either side separately, incised, sutured and tied with #0 chromic catgut suture. In the midline the bladder was further sharply dissected down using a scalpel again removing a little more of the myome-trium and at this point it appeared that we were close to the vagina in the midline and there was entered using a sharp scalpel.

Certainly the vaginal cavity was entered without difficulty and the right corner was then clamped across using a Roger's forceps. In opening the vagina from the top, it was clear that a longitudinal septum was still present in the vagina and that there were two separate duplex vaginas. The septum was then cut across and the entire specimen was then cut free from the upper vagina. In the left side of the vagina, a large amount of clear mucus and old blood drained into the abdominal cavity and this had obviously been an obstructed hydrohematocolpos on this left side.

At this point, both corners of the vault were sutured with a figure-of-eight #0 chromic catgut suture and anchored to the uterosacral ligament pedicle. The vault was then whipped open using #0 chromic catgut suture, and whipping over the septum of the vault as well so that we had a figure –of-eight configuration of cuff with the septum in the midline of the two vaginal openings.

At this point, some bleeding points were over sewn using #3 chromic catgut suture on the anterior aspect of the vaginal vault where we had sharply dissected away the bladder, the myometrial tissue adjacent to the bladder was resutured to the vault tissue with two figure-of-eight sutures. Following this, no arterial bleeding was noted although there was some slow oozing from the tissues on the under-surface of the bladder so therefore a ½" Penrose drain was placed through the right side of the vagina and split in the middle such that both right and left arms were draining the right and left aspects of the pelvis.

At this point the pelvic peritoneum was closed with #2 chromic catgut sutures, and the abdomen was then closed in the usual way running the anterior abdominal peritonea with #0 chromic catgut sutures. When we were ready to close the rectus fascia it was obvious that there was a hole in the dome of the bladder. This must have taken place at the entry to the abdomen where the bladder may have been thinned and then pulled open by the pressure of our abdominal retractor. In any case the dome of the bladder was clearly identified and was opened and was then closed with a three layer closure of #3-0 Vicryl suture running three individual layers, the first one closing the bladder sub mucosa to sub mucosa.

Following closure of the bladder, a few bleeding points were cauterized on the rectus muscles, and the rectus fascia was then closed with a running stick of # 0 Dexon. The subcutaneous layer was then approximated in the midline with #0 Dexon and the skin was then closed using staples and Steri-Strips.

In summary, this is a 37 year old female who was born with several congenital anomalies. She has had repeated surgeries in the past and at this point underwent a total abdominal hysterectomy of a bicornuate uterus, a left salpingo-oophorectomy was carried out for a hematohydrosalpinx on the left side. The right ovary and tube were preserved. There was a 1 ½ cm physiologic cyst in the right ovary which was left and at the time of hysterectomy the vagina was found to be duplex and the left side of the vagina contained a significant amount of old dark mucus suggesting that it was not draining well from below. This will have to be addressed at a future date. I should also mention that the dome of the bladder was opened at the time of surgery inadvertently but this was recognized and closed in a three layer closure of #2-0 Vicryl suture.

Estimate blood loss at surgery was about 500 cc. The patient was stable throughout the procedure and the instrument and sponge counts were correct. The patient awakened in the operating room and was taken to PAR in good condition.

End of Report

—

September 12, 1989 Examination Notes Dr. C.W. Carpenter to Dr. P. Quelch

Just a note regarding Patty Emry who we examined on August 31, 1989. Patty still notes some vaginal bleeding which occurs after intercourse, and sometimes simply after running. She also notes a left-sided pain which tends to be associated with eating. The voiding pattern is satisfactory; however, she has decreased her fitness effort because of the bleeding.

On physical examination the abdomen was flat and muscular. The discomfort was pointed lateral, and just above the umbilicus on the left side.

Pelvic examination revealed there is a mucoid bloody discharge from the upper vault area. I did not see any significant granulation tissue.

Cultures and sensitivities were taken from the vault and I treated the area with silver nitrate, in an effort to settle the bleeding. My thoughts are to ask Patty to return in approximately ten days, and to consider whatever other steps are needed to improve the vault of the vagina. The vault itself appears to be adequately supported, but does seem to be involved in a low grade or irritant effect in the upper vagina.

Perhaps this is a reflection in the area of the upper vagina which was revealed at the time of the hysterectomy. We will reassess the situation in 10 days.

—

September 15, 1989 Examination Report Dr. C.W. Carpenter to Dr. P. Quelch

She attended on September 8, 1989. A culture from the vagina has shown Group B Streptococci. She had negative urine. She does however; still complain of mid abdominal pain. I'm not certain whether this is abdominal pain or not. The left pain is slightly above the flank. However, she is concerned regarding the persistence of this discomfort and accordingly I am going to arrange for an IVP. If this is clear I will ask Patty to follow up with you for further evaluation of the abdominal aspects. In the meantime, I am establishing her on Penicillin G orally to treat the B Streptococcus.

—

October 17, 1989 Examination Report Dr. C.W. Carpenter to Dr. P. Quelch

Patty attended on October 13, 1989. She had been seen and assessed by Dr. Ankenman at my request. This was to evaluate the findings of an IVP which suggested some change in the middle, lobe and the left kidney. Patty had a difficult time with Dr. Ankenman, and I think it would be appropriate if we organized a second opinion probably from Dr. Sec Chan.

—

February 1, 1990 VGH Dr. C.W.Carpenter Pelvic Mass, Large Hemorrhagic cystic right ovary/ Laparoscopy, Laparotomy with right Oophorectomy.

History: This patient is a 39 year old para 3 who underwent hysterectomy in April 1989 with a left oophorectomy at that time. Since that time she has had intermittent spotting especially associated with intercourse. The patient was referred to the Emergency Room on January 24 complaining of two day history of persistent lower abdominal pain and cramping. The patient is known to have congenital bowel defects which required a pull through operation as an infant. Since that time she has required use of enemas to maintain bowel function. Other than that the patient had no complaints of changes in her normal bowel habits. There was no vaginal discharge. She complained of a small amount of nausea on the day of admission but otherwise no other GI complaints. There were no urinary tract infection symptoms.

On examination she was found to have an enlarged mass in the area of the cul-de-sac.

The patient was admitted to VGH where she underwent ultrasound, barium enema and IVP. The mass appeared to rise in the area between the bladder and the rectum. Decision was made for laparoscopy and possible laparotomy. On the 1st of February the patient was taken to the operating room.

Procedure and Findings: Under general anesthetic the patient was prepped and draped in a semilithotomy position. The bladder was catheterized. The patient was examined under anesthetic and a large cystic mass was palpated in the area of the cul-de-sac. Following this a small subumbilical incision was made through which a Verres needle was inserted and after checking the location, approximately 3.5 litres of CO_2 were insufflated. A trocar followed by laparoscope was then introduced with no complications. A manipulating probe was inserted through a suprapubic incision.

The small bowel was seen to be quite adherent in the area of the cul-de-sac. We were unable to move the small bowel forward in order to get a good look at the mass in the cul-de-sac. The decision was then made to proceed with laparotomy.

The patient was then reprepped and draped in the usual fashion. A Pfannenstiel incision was made removing the old scar. This was carried through subcutaneous tissue to rectus fascia. The rectus fascia was incised transversely and dissected off the rectus muscle. The rectus muscle was then split in the midline and the peritoneal cavity was entered.

Again the small bowel was seen to be densely adherent in the pelvis. By moving some loops of small bowel a large hemorrhagic cystic ovary was seen. Using blunt dissection the bowel was dissected off the surface of the cystic ovary. This was carried out until the attachment of the ovary and the ovarian ligament was identified. At this point the pedicle was clamped, cut and doubly legated with #0 chromic. The ovary was approximately 8 cm in diameter and cystic and hemorrhagic.

Inspection of the small bowel following this revealed that the area where the bowel had been bluntly dissected from the ovary was somewhat raw but there was no real active hemorrhage. Hemostasis was quite good. In the area of the terminal ileum just before the junction with the cecum there was a knuckle of bowel noted with lumen on either side being quite stenosed, approximately 1 cm in diameter. An intraoperative consultation was made to a general surgeon (Dr. Allardyce) who inspected the small bowel and decides that no further surgery to the bowel should be carried out at this time. He did note that the terminal portion of the ileum just proximal to the knuckle was somewhat dilated and hypertrophied. This is likely from longstanding problem with this small lumen.

At this point hemostasis was checked and seen to be good. The pelvis was thoroughly flushed with warm normal saline. The abdomen was then closed in the usual fashion, #0 chromic to peritoneum, #0 Dexon to fascia, 2-0 Dexon to subcutaneous tissue and Steri-Strips to skin. A Hemovac drain was placed beneath the fascia and brought out through a separate stab wound adjacent to the incision.

The patient tolerated the procedure well and was taken to the Recovery room in stable condition. Estimated blood loss was 250 cc. An NG tube was placed intraoperatively because of manipulation of the small bowel and the patient will be kept NPO until she has active bowel sounds.

Unfortunately, by the following day, the patient started complaining of increased nausea and retching. Investigations including abdominal x-ray at this time revealed that there was evidence of small bowel obstruction. The patient was placed back on NG suction and intravenous fluids only.

The patient was also followed by surgery for this problem and underwent follow-up abdominal x-rays to monitor the improvement in her obstruction. The NG tube was eventually discontinued again on the 9th postoperative day. She tolerated this well and in fact, had no further problems. X-rays revealed that the obstruction had almost completely resolved.

The only other complication was a urinary tract infection the patient developed around postoperative day 12, and was started on ampicillin orally.

The patient was discharged home in good condition on her 13th postoperative day on February 14, 1990, to be followed up by both Dr. Carpenter and Dr. Quelch.

—

March 22, 1990 Report Dr. M.G. Clay to Dr. P.C. Quelch

You will be aware that I saw Mrs. Emry while she was hospitalized recently. There was concern that she might have a small bowel obstruction but in fact I felt that she had a prolonged ileus after her surgery and conservative treatment was successful.

When Mrs. Emry was in to see Dr. Carpenter on March 12th I saw her as well. Apparently I had suggested to her that contrast studies might be done following her hospital discharge and resumption of normal activities. She was so well and completely asymptomatic when I examined her that I feel now nothing further is the only appropriate route.

Should Mrs. Emry develop any more further difficulties with her bowel, of course one would start from the beginning again, recognizing her long term disability with the original problem of imperforate anus. She is back to her regular adjustment of enemas and so I think that she should just be left at that.

—

August 20, 1990 Examination Report Dr. M.G. Clay to Dr. P.C. Quelch

Thank you for asking me to see Mrs. Emry who came back for examination August 24th concerned about some left lower quadrant pain. As you know, the patient has congenital abnormalities with her disability resultant from originally an imperforate anus and repair. This has resulted in requiring enemas daily to clear her bowel. In the last while the patient has been travelling and the result was that she had been unable to look after her bowel function satisfactorily so that she managed to get a little build up and discomfort.

Since her recent hospitalization the patient has been eating bran which helps her to be more regular in her general situation which is not terribly bad. However, the patient does have some difficulties with constipation now and also some pain in her back. She herself wondered if some of her symptoms were being reinforced by the current tension regarding her husband's lack of employment.

While I examined the patient I really felt that there was nothing wrong with regard to her bowel and have informed her of that. She was being seen by Dr. Carpenter at the same time and I am sure he will be in touch with you directly.

—

September 6, 1990 Examination Report Dr. C.W. Carpenter to Dr. P. Quelch

Just a note regarding Patty Emry who attended on August 24, 1990. She was having pain in the LLQ. This appeared to be precipitated when she bent to the left or bent forward. It seemed to be more in her back.

She notes that voiding is satisfactory. Bowel movements are not always complete and she frequently has gas. She utilized enemas as previously, and has noted some variations there.

At the present time, she is not doing any athletics and is somewhat distressed regarding the family situation, as her husband Greg is not working at the present time.

The pain appears to be up and down her back and quite muscular in nature.

Premarin, 0.625 mg. is utilized on a daily basis for 25 days out of each month.

Physical examination showed a well-looking patient. On abdominal examination the abdomen was flat. The loins were clear. The colon was palpable but it was not enlarged, and it was not acutely tender. The pelvic examination showed normal external genetalia. There was some mucoid fluid at the upper vault, but those tissues appeared normal. There were no masses felt and on recto-vaginal examination the adnexal areas felt basically clear. There was no buildup of fluids and the whole area felt basically as a normal post-operative situation.

My impression was that of primarily back spasm and possibly a spinal effect which was feeding forward into the anterior aspect of the abdomen.

From a gynecological standpoint, she appeared to be in a steady and satisfactory state. Dr. Graham Clay assessed her bowel at the same time, and felt that this was normal as well.

—

October 22, 1991 Examination Report Dr. W. L. Brown to Dr. P. Quelch Lipoma Consultation

I recently saw Patty Emry, a 40 year old woman who has a lipoma beneath the shoulder, along the posterior axillary fold. This has been present for a number of years and has not undergone any recent changes suggestive of malignant degeneration.

Certainly on examination she has a smooth-walled non-fixed lipoma.

I have discussed the possibility of removing this with her and I am in agreement with here that liposuction would be the most appropriate way of dealing with this. I pointed out to her that unfortunately the government does not cover the cost of removing lipomas by liposuction although curiously enough they will cover it if an open technique is used. At any rate she didn't seem particularly bothered and wanted some reassurance about its benign nature and after discussing this, we have agreed to simply leave it.

—

December 27, 1991 Examination Report Dr. D.J. Matzinger to Dr. P. Quelch

X-ray report of Dorsal Spine, Left Ribs

A minimal lower dorsal curvature convex to the right is noted. The paraspinal soft tissues are normal appearing. Minor early degenerative changes are noted at D 8 through 12 with marginal osteophytes detected along the lateral and anterior vertebral margins. This is associated with some irregularity and minor sclerotic changes of the vertebral end plates D 9 through 12. No areas of bony destruction are noted and the pedicles are intact.

No rib fracture or areas of boney destruction are noted.

Impression is of minor early changes of degenerative disc disease are noted in the lower spine at D 8 through 12.

—

December 31, 1991 Examination Report Dr. E.L. Tanton to Dr. P. Quelch

Ultrasound Abdominal Sonogram

Both kidneys are normal with respect to size and position measuring approximately 9.5 and 10.6 cms. In maximal length on the right and left sides respectively. Slight lobulation of the renal contours is noted bilaterally however, normal renal cortical thickness is preserved on either side. No evidence of hydronephrosis, renal calcification or mass lesion is seen.

The gallbladder and biliary tree, liver, spleen, pancreas and aorta are normal.

A cursory scan of the pelvis, with nondistended bladder, revealed a rounded 3 cm. echogenic mass along the left side of the bladder wall, projecting into the bladder lumen. The significance of this finding is patient with multiple previous surgeries and nondistended bladder is uncertain. An additional echo poor "mass-like" lesion is noted in the position of the rectum. This could represent fecal debris.

Impression: A slight lobulation of the renal contours may be on a basis of minor scarring although renal cortical thickness is normally maintained. A follow up pelvic ultrasound, with full bladder, is recommended for further evaluation of an apparent mass related to the wall of the urinary bladder.

—

February 12, 1992 Richmond General Hospital P. Quelch, F. Mondor

Diagnostic Imaging Report

Examination of the chest revealed the heart and mediastinal structures are within normal limits. No active intrapulmonary process is identified.

Supine and upright views of the abdomen have been obtained. The bowel gas pattern shows a few air fluid levels which appear to lie within relatively normal caliber bowel. While this may represent early partial obstruction and entity such as gastroenteritis or even recent enema can give this appearance. If clinically warranted a further examination in 23 to 48 hours could be obtained. There is a small calculus demonstrated in the right intercostal vertebral angle and this could represent calcification within kidney, adrenal or pancreas or perhaps gallbladder and if clinically appropriate an ultrasound is recommended for further evaluation. No other abnormality is demonstrated.

Impression is a few air fluid levels are demonstrated within the abdomen and while this may represent an early partial small bowel obstruction a gastroenteritis or even recent enema preparation could give this appearance.

A small calcific radiodensity is evident in the right costovertebral angle and ultra sound is recommended for further evaluation.

—

March 6, 1992 Examination Report Dr. R.H. Irish to Dr. P. Quelch

Ultrasound Pelvic Sonogram with no significant abnormality apparent.

—

December 8, 1992 Examination Report Dr. V.J. Vail to Dr. P. Quelch

Ultrasound Pelvic Sonogram with no significant abnormality identified.

—

March 12, 1993 Examination Report Dr. D.A. Dolden to Dr. P. Quelch

Diagnostic Imaging Report

A bilateral mammography examination. The small palpable density in the left areolar area was marked using a metallic density. Even on microfocus magnification study the apparent palpable density could not be demonstrated satisfactorily. Ultrasound is recommended for further evaluation. Otherwise the appearance of the breast parenchyma is unremarkable. No clustered microcalcification or architectural distortion is demonstrated.

Impression: Small palpable density in the left areolar area could not be imaged as a discrete entity. Ultrasound is recommended for further evaluation.

The mammographic study does not demonstrate evidence suggestive of malignancy. Assuming the investigation of the palpable density leads to benign cause, annual screening mammography is advised.

—

March 13, 1993 Examination Report Dr. V.J. Vail to Dr. P. Quelch

Diagnostic Imaging Report

Left Breast Sonogram. Comparison was made to mammogram of March 11, 1993. The left breast was carefully examined using high frequency small parts ultrasound transducer. Specific attention was paid to the areolar/subareolar region. No discrete cystic or solid mass is identified within the left breast.

Impression: Negative examination. If there are any clinically suspicious findings, a negative mammogram or sonogram should not preclude biopsy.

—

July 13, 1993 Vancouver General Hospital Dr. M.L. Primer to Dr. P. Quelch

Surgical Pathology Report, Surgical procedure: Aspiration Biopsy, Breast

Left breast aspirate (fine needle). The smear is acellular and not suitable for interpretation. K. Suen, MD, Comment: Strictly speaking this aspirate is insufficient for diagnosis. However, a dense fibrous nodule in fibrocystic disease can give rise to a similar cytologic picture. Clinical and radiological correlation is requested.

—

August 23, 1993 Examination Report Dr. M. Primer to Dr. P. Quelch

Opinion: Mrs. Emry has a tender lump in her left breast which is almost certainly benign. I think it is an area of cystic mastitis and I would not recommend that she have an open biopsy unless the findings progress. In fact she is feeling better in the last six weeks with less tenderness.

She also has a five centimeter lipoma on the posterior aspect of the right axilla. I have discussed with her the options of having it excised surgically or removed through liposuction. She has decided to go ahead with having it surgically removed and will arrange to do this late November early December after the volleyball season.

—

August 30, 1994 Examination Report Dr. M.F. Jenkins to Dr. P. Quelch

Diagnostic Imaging Report

Bilateral Mammograms comparison to March 11, 1993 showed no interval change apparent.

Impression: Bilateral mammograms demonstrating no evidence of malignancy. Follow up mammogram is recommended in one year's time.

—

August 31, 1994 Examination Report - Dr. F.G. Braig to Dr. P. Quelch

Otolaryngology

The above patient is a Physical Education teacher and at the present time she is running a volleyball camp and is finding her voice deteriorating and it gets worse the more she uses it, particularly when she has to raise her voice during sporting activities or instruction periods. She has had problems with her voiced in the past and seems to get worse whenever she get excited or is carrying on some instruction during coaching services. In the past she has been a singer but she finds she can't sing anymore and she has had a lot of other professions as an artist, mother, etc. She has had a lot of medical problems including a lot of gynecological surgery and medical problems in that regard. At the present time she is on estrogen but no other medications. She is allergic to bee stings. She has a history of heartburn but no significant reflux.

Indirect laryngoscopy was impossible to visualize her larynx because of its nature and anatomy so I did a fiberoptic laryngoscopy and she has a small vocal cord nodule on the left vocal cord, suggestive of vocal abuse.

I reassured her about my findings that this is an entirely benign condition and is likely callas on the vocal cords from overuse or abuse and she should just relax about her talking a bit more and use amplification whenever necessary to raise the intensity of her speaking. Portable microphones are available and should be used in her situation. If this doesn't help her after 2 or 3 months of trying simple assistance, she should probably be seen at the VGH Voice Lab and a referral would have to be put through for that if necessary.

—

March 8, 1995 Examination Report Dr. F.G. Braig to Dr. P. Quelch -Otolaryngology

Examination showed a broadly sessile nodule on her left cord. The mobility was normal. On phonation, she had significant bulging of her external jugular veins. Otherwise, the remainder of the ENT examination was unremarkable.

Conclusion: She has vocal cord nodules due to chronic voice abuse.

Recommendation: I suggested to her to get voice instructions to get her out of her faulty voice pattern. If she is not making head way we should do a microlaryngoscopy with removal of the nodule. She will get in touch with the voice teacher.

—

July 18, 1996 Examination Report -Dr. F.G. Braig to Dr. P. Quelch

Otolaryngology

When I saw her last year, she had a small broadly sessile vocal cord nodule on the left side but today I could not see any lesion on her cords. The remainder of the ENT examination was unremarkable.

Conclusion: She still has spastic dysphonia.

Recommendation: I suggested to her to be seen at the Voice Clinic at VGH and will make an appointment for her.

1995 Right hip surgery to remove a fatty tumor, and examination to check for skin cancer on back of left knee, benign.

—

August 30, 1995 Examination Report Dr. S. C. Brady to Dr. P. Quelch

Lipoma right axilla and multiple moles.

This 44 year old woman was in the office today for assessment of a lipoma on the right axilla area which has been present for many years. She also had slowly growing nevi on the right lip, the right cubital fossa and the left hip area which she would like to have removed as well.

Examination: There is a 6 to 7 mm, firm, rubbery lipoma on the right axilla area which feels lobulated under the skin. I suspect that there is a fairly significant fibrous component to this.

There are benign nevi located on the right lower lip, the cubital fossa and the left hip area.

All of these can be removed in the Out Patient Department under local anesthetic. The scars were explained and she understands that they are not totally predictable and she accepts this. I would do two sessions one for the lipoma and the other for the nevi.

—

October 16, 1995 Operative Report Dr. S. C. Brady to Dr. P. Quelch

Removal and layered flap closure right lower lip and left hip and excision and cauterize right antecubital fossa lesion.

The patient was taken to the Ambulatory Care Room and sequentially each of the areas of the lower face, the right antecubital fossa, and left hip were prepped with Hibidil and draped in a sterile manner.

On the lower lip, the nevus was outlined with an elliptical excision oriented vertically with the top of the incision being just at the skin vermilion junction. The area was infiltrated with a small amount of 2% Xylocaine with 1:1000ths of Adrenalin and Bicarb. The lesion was excised down to subcutaneous/muscular layer. Because of gaping, it was necessary to create advancement flaps and these were done with the scalpel utilizing dermal cutbacks. Bleeding was controlled with fine electrocoagulation. The deep dead space was closed and flaps were advanced forward and held with 6-0 Vicryl suture, knots buried. The skin was then closed with 6-0 fast-absorbing gut suture under no tension. Steri-Strips completed this portion.

In the right atecubital fossa region, the mole was infiltrated and simply excised down to the subdermal level. A few bleeding points were coagulated. A light dressing applied.

On the left hip region, a dermatofibroma was outlined with a transverse incision following the skin tension lines. The area was infiltrated and the lesion excised down to the subcutaneous fatty tissue. There was significant stretching and pulling on the wound, so further advancement flaps were created with the scalpel utilizing dermal cutbacks as well. Bleeding was controlled with electrocoagulation. The deep dead space was closed and flaps were advanced forward and held with 4-0 Vicryl suture, knots buried. This allowed the skin to be closed with a running subcuticular 4-0 Prolene suture. A light dressing was applied. Wound instructions were given and the patient asked to call for an appointment to have the hip suture out next week.

Specimens from each of the three areas were taken, and analyzed by the Richmond Hospital Laboratory. Diagnosis: skin excisions from lower lip, right knee, and left hip all showing benign intradermal nevi.

—

1998 Severed left Achilles, surgery to repair, off work for four months.

October 17, 1998 Operative Report Dr. S. Lui to Dr. P. Quelch

Complete tear of the left Achilles tendon/ Repair

With the patient in the prone position, local anesthetic of 2% Xylocaine was given around the defect of the Achilles tendon tear, after which the leg was then properly prepped and draped in the usual fashion. A pneumatic tourniquet was then inflated above the knee.

Incision over the rupture of the Achilles tendon was made and deepened down through the skin and subcutaneous tissue. The peritenoneum was incised and indeed, identifying a couple ruptures of the Achilles tendon. This was irrigated and cleaned. The ends could be reapproximated and therefore, a Bunnell type of suture was used with a Keith needle threading through it and tightened, after which 2-0 Dexon was used to complete the repair on both ends until a secure repair was then noted.

3-0 was used to repair the peritenoneum completely and then 4-0 subcuticularly. Steri-Strips were applied to the skin. The wound was then properly padded and dressed in the usual fashion. The patient was then put in the supine position and the cast completed with the knee in about 45 degrees of flexion.

The patient was then taken to the Recovery Room in satisfactory condition without any complications.

—

1999 Heart palpitations – three hour tests at St. Paul's, irregularly occur.

September 16, 1999 Cardiology Examination Dr. C. Gailey to Dr. P. Quelch

Symptoms of Occasional Palpitations accompanied by dyspnea and chest heaviness.

Mrs. Emry described about six episodes of palpitations in the past six years. One episode occurred while she was playing golf. She felt a very rapid pounding in her chest, not necessarily accompanied by other symptoms. Other episodes have occurred while bending over and sometimes seem to be precipitated by alcohol, only in small amounts. The last few episodes have been accompanied by a feeling of being unable to catch her breath as well as anterior chest pressure. Episodes generally last about five minutes. During one episode of palpitations, she used her mother's heart monitor and BP Cuff. Pulse was measured at 72 but the BP was low.

Usually she is quite physically active, working as a physical education instructor. Since she severed here Achilles tendon a few months ago, activity level has dropped and she has gained some weight. However, she has not experienced chest pain or dyspnea on exertion nor at rest. She has had two dizzy spells but these were not associated with the palpitations (she does not become dizzy with palpitations). She has not had other cardiac type symptoms such as complete syncope, orthopnea, PND, or ankle edema.

Cardiovascular Risk Factors: She has never smoked. Her father has a cardiac problem which Mrs. Emry described as a fast heart beat. Apparently, he has had this since he was young. There is no family history of angina. Mrs. Emry does not have hypertension and is not diabetic. Cholesterol has not been checked, to her knowledge.

Physical Examination: On examination she was a healthy woman in no physical distress. BP was 120/80 and pulse was 70 and regular. Head and neck exam was normal. Chest was clear. Cardiac exam was normal with no gallops or murmurs heard. There is no ankle edema.

Stress test was performed. She exercised for 12 minutes of the Bruce protocol, achieving a heart rate of 172 and completing 13.4 METS. The test was stopped due to fatigue and achievement of target heart rate. There was no chest pain. BP rose normally to 180/80. With exercise, there were 2 mm of flat to up sloping ST depressions in the inferior leads most obviously and lesser ST depressions in the lateral precordial leads. ST segments remain saggin for at least 5 minutes of recovery.

Interpretation: Normal exercise tolerance, clinically negative for angina and electrocardiographically suggestive of ischemia.

Holter Monitor Recording: Holter showed sinus rhythm at a rate of 74 with 1 atrial run of 6 beats which was asymptomatic. There were only 12 other PAC's and 9 PVC's i.e. insignificant ectopy and no pauses.

Impression and Plan: It is difficult to determine the cause of Mrs. Emry's palpitations as they are so infrequent and will unlikely be captured by monitored. As they are short lived, infrequent and not associated with severe symptoms, no further work up will performed at this time. The ST depressions on stress test are concerning, however, as she is a young woman with no other cardiac risk factors. This certainly could be false positive, however, at the age of 48 a stress MIBI will be ordered to clarify this. I would be pleased to see her after the MIBI. In the meantime, fasting lipid profile has been ordered.

Q5000 Stress Test Summary showed good exercise tolerance. Clinically negative for angina, electrocardiographically positive for ischemia. Scintigraphy pending.

—

2001 GI Problems – Vancouver General Hospital –

Dr. Anderson

October 28, 2001 Examination Report Dr. F.H Anderson to Dr. P. Quelch

Division of Gastroenterology

Thank you for having me assess this patient. She has a very complicated past history and actually is functioning fairly well. It seems that she was born with imperforate anus and had surgery almost immediately upon birth. She apparently had problem having bowel movement required anal dilation and requires enemas. She also was found to have an imperforate vagina, which required multiple surgeries in her early teens. She is subsequently had a cesarean section hysterectomy nephrectomy. She had extensive investigations in January of 1990 when she had her gynecological surgery.

Presently the patient requires enemas to have a bowel movement. The stools themselves have never contained any blood. If she misses having an enema she gets abdominal distention bloating subsequently nausea or vomiting.

Patient is otherwise fairly well. She has no upper GI complaints such as indigestion, heartburn, nausea, or vomiting except as mentioned. She has no other particular symptoms at present.

I obtained this patient's previous records including investigation dating back to 1976. At this point I can't really think of any major intervention. She has become enema dependant to have a bowel movement part of this may relate to her congenital abnormality and part of all her subsequent surgeries. There is little one can do to change this pattern. One can try the usual things such as Modulon and Motilium but I doubt that these would materially change her present status. She is concerned about the future but one can't predict, she has been relatively stable for some time. I think therefore that in the absence of any other symptoms she should probably continue as is certainly if things change we could reassess the situation.

—

July 31, 2007 Examination Report - Dr. J. Nasmith to Dr. P. Quelch

Cardiologist St. Paul's Hospital

The suggestion of supraventricular arrhythmias appears to be present but in such a benign version that I don't believe we are dealing with something that requires any intervention at this point in time.

As you know, the inconvenience, costs and side effects of medication are not negliable so that when the arrhythmia is un-related to any health hazard it is hard to justify prescriptions for this amount of ectopy.

I would continue reassurance with the understanding that her unusual bowel predicament could lead to a host of sensations that would not respond to our therapies. If she has recurrence of the very unpleasant sustained and rapid rate such as skiing produced last winter, we would have to reexamine things from the point of view using Valsalva or gag reflex, or possibly the pill-in-pocket routine to keep her from having to spend too much time in ER.

Some patients are so uncomfortable during these sensations that they insist on some kind of remedy but hundreds of dollars of medications and two pills a day for the rest of life, to avoid possibly one or two episodes a year is not what most of like doing. So hang tight and with a bit of luck, she will not be particularly uncomfortable but a day may come when age wear and tear changes her overall profile.

—

August 9, 2007 Examination Report Dr. M. Fishman to Dr. P. Quelch

Gastroenterology

Mrs. Emry continues to require an enema nightly in order to feel that she empties her rectum sufficiently to avoid abdominal cramps. Without this, she is not able to sleep through the night. Back last spring, she was having shooting abdominal pains, worse when she would bend over, accompanied by acid reflux. This has improved considerably on Nexium which she takes most days. She also has a lot of posprandial abdominal bloating, pain, borborygmi and flatulence, especially after certain foods like pizza, or if she is under stress. Cheese or milk do not bother her otherwise. Gravol seems to help, and she is also better if she can run for exercise. During this time she has gained some weight. It seems as though she also has had palpitations diagnosed as some form of supraventricular tachycardia which has been cleared by the cardiologist who attributed to her gastrointestinal problems. This may be reflex tachycardia secondary to abdominal pain. The abdominal pain sometimes radiates to her back.

Opinion and Recommendations: In summary, she continues to have symptoms of dysfunctional bowel. I discussed dietary issues again. She is really not keen on having surgery and I would agree that would be absolutely a last resort. As long as her cardiologist is not concerned about potential harm from the intermittent arrythmias that may be aggravated by her gastrointestinal symptoms, I do not have any particular concern was that it would be dangerous otherwise. This is simply a matter of having unpleasant and inconvenient symptoms. There is probably not much else that we offered at present.

2007 Heart palpitations, tests completed without solution. Extreme pain both knees – Dr. Taunton – needed to lose weight and strengthen quads.

November 7, 2007 Examination Report Dr. N Prasad to Dr. P. Quelch

Early degenerative changes both knees including patellofemoral joint but also additional degenerative medial meniscal tear left knee.

X-rays of both knees show slight narrowing of the patellofemoral compartment as well as mild narrowing of the medial. She has an old bony ossicle off the medial aspect of the right femoral condyle likely from her old ligament sprains.

On examination her standing leg alignment is fairly neutral with good static arch height. She is able to walk with comfortable gait but does have some discomfort in the left knee on full squat. There is no effusion but there is slight fullness towards the popliteal region of the left more than right knee. There is no palpable Baker's cyst. Ligamentous testing of the knees is stable. On palpation, she has pain towards the patellar facets of both knees with increased pain on patellar compression maneuver. The left knee also has increased pain over the medial joint line compared to the right with mild pain on McMurray but no click.

Management: I think Patty has some evidence of early degenerative changes in both knees, especially the patellofemoral joint. However, the recent injury with golf a few months ago may have also caused a degenerative tear of her medial meniscus. Symptoms have been better in the past few weeks with the use of Advil and she's been able to get back to running. Therefore I think it is reasonable to hold off arthroscopy. We will get her to do more cycling and see if she can add some strengthening with wall squats progressing towards quarter squats. End of Report

End of Reports

Acknowledgments

It is important to thank the medical community who continue to make strides improving patient treatments and care. Thanks to my friends within the medical profession, especially Lynn and Derrick, and my other doctors who gave me insight into my surgical history. All of you took time out of your busy lives to read the first drafts and I know that was above and beyond the call of duty.

Next, a huge thank you to my editor Bernice Lever, a published poet and editor in residence with the Canadian Authors Association – Vancouver. She was patient and candid about my writing style.

I am relieved to have found the GI Society and Badgut.org. I appreciate the wonderful staff who I speak with frequently. I want to thank these professionals for their sensitivity. I know they are not going to say, "Eww, you do what?" If you know anyone with gastro-intestinal issues, who may need advice and information to help live a better and more active life, be sure to check out www.Badgut.org website. They have printed resources on numerous health issues found online. These resources have helped my specific queries of IBS, acid reflux or GERD and diet. I am amazed at the breadth of resources: Doctors advice, education pamphlets and videos, BadGut Basics, Lecture Series and the Inside Tract newsletter.

I am so grateful to my friends and colleagues who reviewed the first drafts of 'It Takes A Sense of Humour'. I cherish your comments and suggestions, especially Vicky for giving up part of a holiday and hours of edits correcting my scribble. All of your opinions and excitement over the book spurred me on.

Sitting at my computer for hours I would frequently hear that, "You've got mail." and it would be past students or Facebook supporters sending me positive messages, dance videos or a good joke to pick up my mood. Thanks for the fun, music and laughter,

To my family, they kept encouraging me to continue on and finish the story. When I started to write this memoir I was concerned how they would feel about the end result. It was no surprise, they are all excited about this process, and their gentle prodding motivated me daily, 'Get out of bed and get this done!' Thanks to my older brother and sister-in-law who after listening to some of my memories suggested I write my stories down. My siblings have never been negative with me, and I am blessed to have them in my life.

I am so grateful for my children's patience love and support during this process even when my fears would rise up and I would ask, "Should I do this and will this book embarrass them?"

Lastly to my lover, best friend and ghost writer Greg, he has been on my journey and experienced first hand the last 44 years. I love this man, he makes me listen and think daily, 'Oh my gosh, I am so lucky and proud to be alive!'

To my twin Cathy, I will see you, hopefully not too, soon. Look for me; I am the short

one at the pearly gates holding up the line trying to make St. Peter laugh! Once again the O'Leary twins will be together. Heaven will be a better place when we are all together.

It Takes A Sense Of Humour!

Our Clan Celebrating Family...We Rock!

Patty and grandson Emry Oliver Rex Aarts

For my twin sister – I told you I was going to live life for the two of us. Family is so very important to us. I am so very proud of our children's love of family, and they are truly dedicated to their partners. What a gift! What a blessing, we are delighted.

I am grateful to my parents who back in 1950 would not let the medical community give up on me and put me on "the shelf". I know that my family knows I will do the same for them. I will not give up the fight for my loved ones to live!

About The Author

With a degree in Physical Education and Art from Central Washington University, Patty O'Leary Emry took a running leap into a teaching and coaching career which she enjoys to this day. A robust combination of faith, family, sport, and a sense of humour has lifted her beyond her physical and emotional limits; this outward focus also serves her deepest passion to encourage and empower others to learn how to "balance forward". A lover of painting, music, and dancing, she lives in Vancouver, British Columbia with the love of her life, Greg Dean Emry.

Printed in Canada